Children Around the Messenger

COMPANIONS OF THE
PROPHET ﷺ SERIES

Children Around the Messenger

COMPANIONS OF THE
PROPHET ☙ SERIES

Nizar Abazah

1 2 3 4 5 6 7 8 9 10

All rights reserved. No part of this publication may be reproduced, stored in a retrieval system or transmitted in any form or by any means – electronic, mechanical, photocopying, recording or otherwise – without written permission from the publisher.

© Light Publishing 2015

Nizar Abazah

Children Around the Messenger

ISBN 978-1-915570-32-1

www.lightpublishing.co.uk

بسم الله الرحمن الرحيم

CONTENTS

DEDICATION	9
INTRODUCTION	11
LINEAGE AND CHILDHOOD OF THE MESSENGER ﷺ	13
Forefathers: Ibrahim ﷺ and Ismail ﷺ	13
Grandfather: Abdul Muttalib	16
Father: Abdullah	19
Wet Nurse: Halima	21
Mother: Amina	23
Uncle: Abu Talib	24
CHILDREN IN THE PROPHET'S ﷺ HOUSEHOLD	27
Zayd ibn al-Haritha	27
Ali ibn Abu Talib	29
Aisha bint Abu Bakr	30
Abdullah ibn Jafar	33
Abdullah ibn Abbas	35
Umama bint Hamza	37
Usama ibn Zayd	38
THE PROPHET'S CHILDREN	41
The Prophets' Sons: Qasim, Ibrahim and Abdullah	41

THE PROPHET'S DAUGHTERS	45
Zaynab	45
Ruqayya	46
Umm Kulthum	48
Fatima al-Zahra	49
THE PROPHET'S 🕌 GRANDCHILDREN	55
Ali's sons: Hasan and Hussain	55
Umamah bint Abu al-As	56
THE PROPHET'S 🕌 STEPCHILDREN	61
Khadija's Children	61
Umm Salama's Children	61
Sawda's Children	62
Umm Habiba's Daughter	63
THE YOUNG COMPANIONS	65
Zayd ibn Thabit	65
Anas ibn Malik	66
Abdullah ibn Umar	69
Amah bint Khalid	70
Abu Umair	70
Muath ibn Afran and Muath ibn Amr	71
Uthman ibn Abu al-As	73
Rafi ibn Amr	75
Laila al-Ghafariya	75
Abdullah ibn Zubair	76
Umair ibn Sad	77
AFTERWORD	81
APPENDIX: General Habits and Sayings of the Prophet 🕌 around Children	83

DEDICATION

*To every father and mother concerned for
their child's wellbeing,
Who hope for them to become righteous
individuals in society.*

INTRODUCTION

"He who does not show kindness to our little ones and does not respect our elders is not one of us." This is what the Prophet of Humanity, Muhammad ibn Abdullah ﷺ, came with. He ﷺ was sent as a mercy to mankind.

The Prophet ﷺ had the best of interactions with the children around him. He lived alongside them, he would guide them and he would teach them. He would hug them, kiss them, pat their heads and joke with them. He ﷺ would smile with them, he would place them on his shoulders or they would join him as he rode his animals on journeys. He would guide them to the best course of action and was never aggressive with them if they made mistakes.

In this book, we will study the lives of children who interacted with the Messenger ﷺ. I have gathered these accounts from various sources in both the Prophetic *sira* and Hadith collections. Only a small number of documents about children's interactions with the Prophet ﷺ have survived. The reports that do remain, however, point to the truth of the matter, and so it is with these small gems that we start our exploration. The findings offer insight into these children's lives with the Prophet ﷺ in their early, later and final stages of childhood. These accounts can provide parents with actual prophetic examples on how to interact with their own children so that they can grow to be righteous members of society.

O Allah make firm our feet so that we walk the path of Your Messenger ﷺ, the seal of the prophets. Benefit us with what You have given us, indeed You are the giver of joy and elevation. There is no strength nor power except with You. All praise belongs to Allah (s), the Lord of the Worlds.

Nizar Abazah

LINEAGE AND CHILDHOOD OF THE MESSENGER ﷺ

It is difficult to compare anyone's childhood with the childhood of the Prophet ﷺ, because Allah chose him and guided him under His own supervision. He ﷺ is considered a protected prophet, the most virtuous messenger of them all.

And yet, Muhammad ﷺ was just a man. He was born and raised just as all others were born and raised. The worldly issues that affected others affected him too; happiness, sadness, wealth, poverty, good and ill health all impacted him. And, just like them, he ﷺ died as they died. He is distinguished from all creation, because he ascended to the honourability of prophethood. Nobody ascends to that level except by Allah's decree. And as such, Muhammad ﷺ was an example of goodness and guidance for others to follow.

Since we are speaking about the children around the Prophet ﷺ, it seems only appropriate to first consider his own childhood and ancestry.

FOREFATHERS: IBRAHIM ﷺ AND ISMAIL ﷺ

The Prophet's full name was Muhammad ibn Abdullah ibn Abd al-Muttalib ibn Hashim ﷺ. His lineage reaches back to Ismail ﷺ, the son of Ibrahim ﷺ, the father of the prophets. Before we can understand Prophet Muhammad ﷺ, we must understand the story of his ancestors, Ibrahim ﷺ and Ismail ﷺ.

Ismail ﷺ had a unique story. Prophet Ibrahim ﷺ traveled with his weaning son, Ismail, and his wife, Hajar, to a place in Mecca which had neither water nor vegetation. By Allah's command, he left them there in severe heat and total isolation. As Ibrahim departed, he uttered a humble *dua* and waited for Allah's response. Hajar stood alarmed and asked Ibrahim, "Who are you leaving us with alone here?" He remained quiet, so she asked him again, "Did Allah command you to do this?" He said in a clear voice, "Yes." She then relaxed and said while turning away, "In that case, He will not allow us to perish."

Hajar's water and provisions soon depleted and she became extremely thirsty. Her heart wrung with pain when she heard her son cry, so she began to run between two nearby hills, Safa and Marwa, to see if she could find someone to rescue them. In desperation, she ran between the hills a total of seven times, only becoming thirstier in the process. Finally, she stopped and lost all hope in being saved by anyone, except Allah.

She sought Allah's protection to release them from their tribulation. Now at her weakest, she stopped to check on her son. Suddenly, water started to burst out from beneath Ismail's feet. It swelled up to the sides of the valley. The water was sweet and luscious, gushing forth as a gift directly from Allah. She was now certain that Allah was watching over her and her son.

One can imagine Hajar's tears mixing with the flowing water as it gushed around her. She scooped it up with her palms to quench Ismail's thirst, washing his body to extinguish the intense heat of their surroundings. Fearing that the water would eventually drain away and be lost, she built a sand perimeter around the water and said, "*Zam* (be still) oh river, *zam*!" From that day on, this spring was named Zamzam. That sanctified water didn't just quench her thirst momentarily, it went on to fill her breast with sweet milk and nourish her baby's lips. And it still provides water to pilgrims to this day.

No time had passed at all when migrating birds began to glide round her, descending on the water to drink. Some passing caravans watched the birds from afar, surprised that there was life in the valley at all because their navigator's experience told them otherwise. Slowly, the people began to explore that place until eventually the tribe of Jurhum settled there. Ismail grew up in their midst and life flooded into the valley.

When Ismail was ten years old, his father Ibrahim ﷺ returned. The family were reunited again, and they all rejoiced at his return. Ibrahim came back to Mecca because he had been tasked by Allah to begin construction of the Kaba. He set about building it according to Allah's design, and Ismail helped him as much as possible. Once he completed it, Ibrahim prostrated to Allah, supplicating for the benefit of the sacred town of Mecca. By Allah's command, Ibrahim had established the town's sanctity by prohibiting the uprooting of trees in Mecca, stopping the hunting of animals and outlawing immoral behaviour.

Ibrahim was pleased with this work. And his heart filled with pride as he observed his son, a young, strong, intelligent boy brimming with intellect, energy and honour. It was at this point that an enormous weight descended upon Ibrahim, one which he could neither avert, nor avoid. Allah was commanding Ibrahim to sacrifice his son, Ismail.

He asked himself, could he sharpen a knife, lay his son down and bring the knife to his neck in the same way one would sacrifice a calf or a sheep? Would he be able to do that? What was Allah's wisdom in doing this? His obedience to Allah was essential to his cause, but he still felt alarmed. He was determined not to be weak, but what would he do if his son fled? And what would Ismail think of all this? Ibrahim spent some time mulling over it. He realised that he had to speak to his son. He called Ismail, sat him down by his side and with a hushed sorrow he asked him, "O my dear son. I saw a dream saying that I would have to sacrifice you. Tell me, what do you think I should do?" Ismail replied, "O my father, do as you are commanded. Allah willing, you will find me patient!"

Ibrahim prayed to his Lord for help and courage. He sharpened his knife as best he could. With their hearts filled with faith and surrender, Ibrahim and Ismail travelled to Mina, near Mecca, to fulfil this strenuous task.

Iblis then appeared to Ibrahim, intent on stopping his obedient actions. Hoping that he would fall into sin, Iblis appealed to Ibrahim's fatherly emotions with false sincerity, "Ibrahim, does it make sense for you to sacrifice your son? He is the apple of your eye. Has anybody before you done this?" Feeling his fatherly pain swell, Ibrahim quickly picked up a stone and threw it at Shaytan. "Be quiet! Cursed be, O outcast." But the sly whisperer only went to Hajar to exploit her motherly vulnerabilities instead.

"Do you know what your husband is doing?" Iblis said to Hajar. "He is going to sacrifice your poor child." Hajar, however, was a believer in the father of all prophets, and she knew that he did not move without Allah's command. She leaned over, picked up a stone and said,

"Cursed be, O deviant one!" Only Ismail remained, and Shaytan wanted to make him flee from his father. But Shaytan's fortune was just the same as with Ismail's parents. The deceiver left, slapping his own face in frustration.

In Mina, it was now time to act. Ibrahim was in distress. He turned his face away from his son fearing that he would weaken if he saw him. He sought Allah's help, and sensing His magnificence, he removed himself from his fatherly feelings. When his son felt his father's hesitation, he said to him, "My dear father. Do not be sad. Place me on my face. Sacrifice me from behind."

His father began to do as his son had suggested and he took out the knife which he had made ready. As he resolved to pass it over his son's neck, the angel Jibril ﷺ suddenly descended from the sky with a large sheep and placed it in front of Ibrahim. Jibril said to him, "Peace be with you, O Prophet of Allah. You have fulfilled the dream."

GRANDFATHER: ABDUL MUTTALIB

Ismail ﷺ grew older and went on to have many children. Centuries passed and eventually the leadership of Mecca fell on Abdul Muttalib, the grandfather of Prophet Muhammad ibn Abdullah ﷺ, whose lineage descended from the offspring of Ismail himself.

The religious set up had changed significantly in Mecca. People had begun worshipping idols instead of Allah, and they had erected more than 300 idols around the Kaba. The well of Zamzam had dried up, having been forgotten over time. There was a dire need to give water to the visiting pilgrims, so sourcing water was an arduous task.

One night, Abdul Muttalib was drifting off to sleep when he saw a strange man he didn't recognise. The man instructed him to dig for Zamzam and showed him to its place. As the leader of Quraysh, he was delighted, as a water well would bring relief to everyone. So the next morning Abdul-Muttalib took his tools and his eight-year-old son, al-Harith, to dig the well. As he dug through the earth, he filled up his bucket. Al-Harith would then take the bucket, empty it outside the mosque and then return to his father.

The Quraysh mocked Abdul Muttalib saying, "Couldn't you find an easier place to dig for the well of Mecca?" He didn't reply, he just continued digging as they watched and laughed. All of a sudden, water gushed out soaking the seating area of the people mocking him. They were dazed and confused. Once more, the well poured out the gift of sweet tasting water.

But soon, because of the blessings conferred upon him, envy built up in the hearts of the Quraysh against Abdul Muttalib. Their envy quickly turned to spite, and the spite turned to plotting. The leaders and elders of the Quraysh revolted against Abdul Muttalib, asserting that the Zamzam well belonged to Mecca and not to him alone. The revolt turned to transgression towards the rightful finder, and so they all agreed that they must travel to a soothsayer to settle the matter.

This soothsayer lived on the borders of the peninsula, so they went to relay their story to her, all agreeing that they would follow her instructions. If she decided that Abdul Muttalib had full rights, they would agree to that. However, if she decided that the well was communal and belonged to everybody, then Abdul Muttalib's sharing of the water would be their right rather than a gesture of his kindness. The latter meant that they could share the water with their self-esteem intact.

The leaders travelled with determination to the soothsayer, yearning to meet her, but it was by no means a short distance, and it made them tired and weak. They soon ran out of water and they found themselves in the middle of the desert. They were all but certain of their impending death.

They even agreed that they should each dig their own grave so that if anyone died at any time, they could bury him. Some of them thought, if only they had stayed in Mecca and accepted that the well belonged to Abdul Muttalib. Was this merely a punishment?

Surprisingly, Abdul Muttalib advised them to travel on in the hope that they would find an opening from Allah on the road. The leaders were not expecting what happened next. Abdul Muttalib's camel had barely taken pace when water began to gush out by the camel's feet. On seeing life return to them when they thought all was lost, they realised that it was a message from the unseen, telling them that the well belonged rightfully to Abdul Muttalib.

The party returned to Mecca with their leader Abdul Muttalib finally enjoying the Quraysh's respect. No one dared debate his status or the well any further. And from that day forth, the pilgrims of Hajj benefited from the well of Zamzam.

Abdul Muttalib thought to himself, "These people would not have stood against me if I had many sons." So before long, he married again and had many more children. In the hope of having more sons than daughters (to strengthen his bargaining power), he made a solemn oath in front of the Quraysh that if Allah blessed him with boys, he would sacrifice one of them to God out of gratitude!

Allah fulfilled Abdul Muttalib's hopes, giving him child after child until he eventually had ten boys. The tenth boy was called Abdullah. It was time for him to keep his promise. Abdul Muttalib was concerned that if he did not fulfill his oath, they would reproach him and question his chivalry.

The leaders of the Quraysh were certain that Abdul Muttalib would not keep his promise and they were watching him closely to see which of his sons he would choose to provide as a sacrifice. They realised though, that he was in earnest when he went to the Kaba to consult the divination box in front of Hubal, an idol of pure red, ruby and gold.

Out of respect, Abdul Muttalib approached the custodian of the idol and requested that the custodian's divine arrows choose one of his ten sons for sacrifice. The custodian chanted a peculiar rhyme as many faces looked on, wondering who would be chosen. At last, and with a pregnant pause, the custodian uttered the name "Abdullah" as the stick fell on him. But Abdullah was the youngest and dearest son to Abdul Muttalib! Saddened at the result, Abdul Muttalib felt a deep pain in his soul, but he felt compelled to fulfil his promise, nonetheless.

The house of Abdul Muttalib was filled with noise and alarm as Abdullah's mother, Fatima bint Amr ibn Aidh al-Makhzumi, was devastated by the news. She already despised the 'gods' of the Quraysh, and she wished for the earth to swallow Hubal and his wretched custodian in its entirety. She was distraught as her beloved son was brought to the Kaba to be bled dry in its forecourts. But her objections and her tears were hopeless. She asked, "How am I alone expected to make this sacrifice?" She prayed to Allah as much as she could, her tears flowing so much that she could barely see.

Abdul Muttalib accompanied his son to the Kaba, as other leaders watched on. They all stood, not out of fear for Abdullah, nor out of love for his father or genuine concern for them both, but because they actually feared that a precedent was being set. If Abdul Muttalib sacrificed Abdullah, this would mean that they too would be obliged to follow suit in the future, if they had ten sons.

With that in mind, they hurried to convince him that his self-imposed oath was not valid by their law or religion, and that it was merely his own personal decision that could easily be undone. One person even suggested, "Could you not save your son by sacrificing an animal as ransom, just as our forefather Ibrahim ﷺ did?" Abdul Muttalib replied, "But that came down from Allah Himself and by His command."

Somebody else said, "Then, let's consult the gods! You can set forward a ransom that will satisfy them." Relieved at the prospect, Abdul Muttalib saw them depart in search of a soothsayer to determine a ransom. The soothsayer asked them, "How much blood money is the recompense for murder?" They said, "Ten camels." She responded, "Go back to your city, bring your companion and ten camels too, then sacrifice them with a knife. Then sacrifice more camels until your companion is satisfied."

So on that memorable day, the elders of Mecca gathered around the Kaba. Abdul Muttalib was inside and had started the divination between his son or the ten camels. The custodian responsible for the arrows again initiated the process, but Abdullah's arrow did not win. They added ten more arrows, but Abdullah's arrow was still unsuccessful. The more arrows they added and the more camels they introduced the more Abdullah's arrow would lose. Until at last, there were 100 camels at stake. Only then did his arrow succeed and the boy was saved. Abdul Muttalib could fulfil his oath. His wife Fatima was ecstatic. Abdul Muttalib brought the camels to the mosque and he too was overjoyed. He began sacrificing them to Allah, and as their blood flowed on the Meccan sands, their meat went on to feed whoever would eat it. The meat was even taken to oases outside Mecca so that wild animals and birds could share in the feast.

FATHER: ABDULLAH

Abdullah came from an honourable lineage and was well versed in business and trade. His father would send him far and wide to learn about life, gain experience and acquire wealth. When he reached adulthood, his father looked for a suitable bride for him from amongst the women of Quraysh. He chose Amina bint Wahb bint Abd Manaf, the best of women in status and lineage. An articulate young woman, Amina was clever and eloquent.

The Quraysh gave their blessing and the two soon married happily. Amina joined Abdullah's home and they began their blessed married life. A few months passed and Abdullah departed with a caravan for business in Syria. These caravans would often travel in the summer and winter seasons for two months at a time. Amina yearned for news of her husband's return. Finally, the caravan arrived, and people returned to their homes, filling Mecca with happiness once again. However, Abdullah was not amongst them. Amina asked after his whereabouts and was struck by the saddest of news. Abdullah had been travelling back to visit his uncle in Yathrib when he suddenly fell gravely ill. His body couldn't bear the illness and he died.

Amina's grief was immense and compounded by the fact that she had discovered she was pregnant. She wondered how she would manage to raise an orphan and how would the baby live without its father? Amina was not the only bereaved, of course. The news had truly shocked Abdullah's father, the leader of Quraysh. The terrible news weighed heavy on Abdul Muttalib's soul. It brought back painful memories of the near sacrifice he had made when Abdullah was a child. Now destiny had overtaken him and there was nothing more to be done. Abdul Muttalib asked himself, was this divine revenge for not fulfilling his original oath? Or was it the wisdom of Allah, beyond his comprehension?

Regardless, Abdul Muttalib had little time to grieve fully. All of Mecca was pre-occupied by an imminent danger from the south. A furious army from Yemen - led by Abraha, the Ethiopian Christian viceroy intent on taking over Mecca - threatened to conquer and raze the Sacred House to the ground. Abraha had built a magnificent church in Sanaa and he demanded that the Hajj pilgrims visit it instead of the Kaba.

The soldiers arrived at the Sanctuary boundaries and began to approach. The Meccans knew that they did not possess any physical means to defend themselves from such an enemy. So rather than see Ibrahim's ﷺ construction toppled before their very eyes, they scattered far into the valleys filled with concern. Before the soldiers of Abraha descended on Mecca though, they decided to rest in the valleys to recover from their long journey. It was there that Abraha received an unexpected request from an unidentified visitor, Abdul Muttalib. He entered with his head held high, and after exchanging only a few words, Abraha realised that Abdul Muttalib was in fact the leader of Quraysh. Abraha anticipated that he had come to ask for clemency, a peace treaty or covenant of some kind. However, Abdul Muttalib had in fact come to complain that Abraha's soldiers had ravaged his camels and he wanted them returned.

Abraha began to mock Abdul Muttalib for what he saw as a ridiculous request. He sarcastically replied, "I thought you had come with genuine concern for what was about to happen to your city. But in fact, you're requesting something insignificant!" Undeterred by Abraha's words, Abdul Muttalib replied, "O warrior! Know well that I am lord and master of my camels. I fear for them, but I do not fear for the House of Allah! Because the House has a Master and Lord who will guard it from your tyranny."

Abdul Muttalib's promise was fulfilled. As he left the camp, swarms of birds circled nearby carrying heated stones in their beaks, ready to pelt the invading army. The pebbles burnt through the flesh of the soldiers, destroying Abraha's army. The Yemeni threat was soon forgotten, and the Quraysh returned home to start life anew.

The new year began and indeed a new era like no other. On Monday 12th Rabi al-Awwal (20th August, 570 AC), Abdullah's son, Abdul Muttalib's grandson, was born. He tenderly picked him up and felt sure that the baby was a sign from Allah after Abraha's demise. Abdul Muttalib looked at his beloved grandson and love instantly filled his heart. He felt mercy wash over him as he beheld this orphan child.

Abdul Muttalib carried his grandson to the Kaba and placed him inside. He performed *tawaf* with him inside, thanking Allah for the blessing he had conferred upon him and recalling his son Abdullah, who he still missed keenly. The people of Quraysh asked, "What did you name him?" He replied, "Muhammad." Surprised that the name was not Abdul Uzza, Abdul Laat or Abd Manaf after their gods, they asked him why he had chosen that name. He replied, "I want people to praise him." And that is precisely what happened.

WET NURSE: HALIMA

Shortly after Muhammad ﷺ was born, a group of women from Bani Saad arrived in Mecca looking for work as wet nurses. Amongst them was Halima bint Abi Dhuayb. It was customary in those days for children to be sent to the desert climes to improve their constitution. And so Halima narrates,

> I departed for Mecca with my husband and little boy, who was still weaning, in the month of Sha'ban. We couldn't sleep a single night because our child was crying from hunger. There was nothing left in my breast to nurse him with. Not even our camel had milk. But we were hopeful that there would be relief.

On arriving in Mecca we discovered that no woman was willing to nurse a baby called Muhammad. He was an orphan and so they couldn't expect payment from his father. Every woman eventually took a child, except for me. When it was time to depart, I said to my husband, "I don't like to return without a child to feed. By Allah, I shall go to that orphan and I shall bring him back with us." Upon returning home I began to nurse him, and my breasts swelled with so much milk that he drank and drank until he was satisfied. Then [my son] took his fill and they both slept.

My husband then went to the camel and found that she too was giving milk! So he milked the she-camel and we drank. We quenched our thirst and we were satisfied. My husband said, "Halima, you have acquired a blessed soul [in that boy]." We only experienced more and more goodness for two years until his weaning came to end.

Muhammad ibn Abdullah grew up with the cleanest of air, drinking the purest of Halima's milk. In just one day, he would grow as much as other child would grow in a month. Muhammad stayed with the tribe of Bani Saad for five years. It was customary to stay for just two years, but Halima persuaded Amina to let him stay and thrive. When Muhammad was five years old, Halima suddenly brought Muhammad back to Amina saying that she did not want to keep him any longer. Amina asked why Halima had had such a change of heart. Halima told her of a bewildering event that had taken place.

She described how two men in white garments had taken Muhammad whilst he was playing with her son near the tribal quarters. The children had explained how they placed Muhammad on the sand, opened up his chest and extracted a black clot from his heart. The men said, "This is for the Shaytan!" They washed his heart in a luminous vessel, placed it back in his body, closed his chest and departed. The children had rushed back to their parents relating the worrying events, and so they all ran back only to find Muhammad pale-faced and scared. Halima picked him up and held him close, asking him what had happened. He offered the same explanation as the other children.

Despite its peculiarity, Amina wasn't entirely surprised by Halima's story because she herself had seen signs in her son unlike any other children. Amina carried Muhammad to his grandfather Abdul Muttalib so that his wet nurse Halima could be paid. He looked at him proudly and remarked, "The handsomeness of the Quraysh, the eloquence of the Banu Saad, and the sweetness of Yathrib!"

MOTHER: AMINA

Muhammad spent the next year with his beloved mother. And even though they were only married for a short time, Amina remembered her husband constantly. The next year, when her son was six years old, Amina left with him for Yathrib to see her brothers and to visit Abdullah's grave. Muhammad stood by his mother's side at his father's grave and felt the keenness of their loss and sadness.

The trip lasted about a month in all, with Muhammad spending time playing with his cousins, swimming and flying pet birds. But it was also to be a farewell trip for Muhammad, bringing with it yet more pain and grief. On her return journey to Mecca, Amina suddenly became very weak and could go no further. She had fallen gravely ill and her body was simply unable to fight her sickness. Tragically, her soul departed soon after. Before she passed, Amina entrusted the care of her child to Umm Ayman, a servant that Amina had inherited from her father.

Umm Ayman returned to Mecca with Muhammad. Abdul Muttalib held him close, feeling his sadness for the loss of his parents, he became especially concerned for him and advised his nurse to take extra care of him. Of course, she would not have needed this advice as her heart was filled with love for Muhammad already and she knew that her duty would be as another mother after Amina's demise.

Abdul Muttalib's love for his grandson only deepened with time. A carpet was placed for the elderly leader of the Quraysh in front of the Kaba. He would sit on it, surrounded by his children and would receive his visitors there. When Muhammad would visit and step on the carpet, his uncles would reprimand him and tell him to move. But Abdul Muttalib would reply, "Leave my child... he knows his place. By Allah he will have a great position one day." People soon recognised the special place Muhammad had in his grandfather's heart and would even fondly call him Muhammad ibn Abdul Muttalib, instead of Muhammad ibn Abdullah.

It was a painful day when Muhammad's grandfather died. An intense sorrow and loneliness took root in Muhammad's heart. His uncles and aunts felt for him, and so his eldest uncle, Abu Talib, Abdullah's brother, took Muhammad into his family home. Despite being financially limited, his uncle did not fail in showering his new guest with kindness. Abu Talib and his wife, Fatima bint Asad, loved Muhammad like their own children. Muhammad in turn was extremely sensitive towards them and would avoid burdening them at all costs.

UNCLE: ABU TALIB

Muhammad was just eight years old when he joined his uncle's home, but he had the best of manners. He tried to eat only a little from Abu Talib's table, so when food was laid out, he would not extend his hand towards the plate. His aunty encouraged him to eat and was surprised at his good health despite his nominal appetite. He would often say he was full after drinking only some cups of Zamzam water.

Abu Talib noticed that if his children ate without Muhammad, they would still feel hungry. But if their cousin Muhammad ate with them, they would feel full. So when he wanted them to eat lunch or dinner, he would tell them to wait until Muhammad joined them. If they drank milk, he would give Muhammad the cup to drink from first, then they would drink from the same cup after him.

As Muhammad ibn Abdullah grew into a young man, he began to accompany his uncle to the Levant for trade. When their caravan travelled to the town of Busra in Syria, Muhammad met a monk there called Bahira. He invited Muhammad's caravan to his monastery to dine with him. Bahira saw clear signs of prophethood in Muhammad, as was foretold in the Gospel and the Torah.

Bahira watched Muhammad closely and asked his uncle many questions to confirm that he was indeed the awaited messenger. At that point,

Bahira turned Muhammad around and felt around his shoulder, here he found an area of raised skin described as the size of a pigeon's egg. This was known as the Seal of Prophethood. Fearing for Muhammad, Abu Talib returned back to Mecca. He stayed in the sanctuary of the Kaba and, as no harm came to him, his uncle soon forgot the story of Bahira.

Muhammad started to enjoy the life of a shepherd with the other children. They would often go out to the valleys of Mecca to help his uncle. As time went on, events occurred that demonstrated how Allah was protecting Muhammad from trouble. Once, his friends went to a wedding on the outskirts of Mecca to relax and enjoy some frivolity, all of which was not entirely innocent. They convinced Muhammad to stay with them. When they rested at a stopping place, Allah sent Muhammad into a deep sleep. In doing so, Allah saved him from witnessing dancing, music and the sinful acts of the *jahiliyya*. Only the heat of the sun woke him, once everybody had departed.

Another time, his aunt and uncle reminded him to attend the celebration of an idol called Bawana, and so he attended begrudgingly. Once he was there however, he was overcome with fear and ran far away. When they caught up with him, Muhammad was agitated and pale-faced. Worried for him, they asked why he had run away. He said, "Every time I approached an idol, a frightening individual would appear warning me away." After that incident, they left him to himself and he never venerated or prostrated to an idol because of it.

Over the next few years, Muhammad would say farewell to his childhood. When he was just fourteen years old, the tribe of Qais attacked Mecca in blatant disrespect to the sanctity of the Kaba. Four intense battles followed over a period of four years. Muhammad participated in these battles to repel oppression from outside forces, mainly by making ready the bows and arrows for battle. As the war finally ended with the enemy despondent, Muhammad began his life as a young man. Eyes in Mecca watched him closely. Little did they know that this young man would soon become the final messenger of Islam ﷺ.

CHILDREN IN THE PROPHET'S 🌿 HOUSEHOLD

ZAYD IBN AL-HARITHA

When young Muhammad married Khadija ﷺ, Zayd ibn al-Haritha was a young slave, not more than eight years of age. Muhammad saw in Zayd a bright and gentle nature shining through, and so he loved him. He felt compassion for Zayd, who had been kidnapped by Bedouins as a young child and brought to the market of Hubashah. There they sold him as a slave to one of Khadija's relatives, who purchased him in her name. The young boy had not had his fill of his mother's love, nor the care of his father and he would often think about them.

But as the days went by, Zayd found comfort in their household, a comfort which brought joy back into his heart. He loved his guardian Khadija, who was like a second mother to him. Then as a wedding gift, Khadija gave Zayd to Muhammad, who soon became a father figure for him.

One day, Muhammad held young Zayd's hand as he walked around the gatherings of Quraysh in their forums. Whenever he approached a group, he would tell them, "This is my son, my inherited." He would often make them acknowledge this and refer to him as "Zayd, son of Muhammad". Zayd lived an easy life in Muhammad and Khadija's house, growing up as a part of the household.

However, Zayd's real mother, father and siblings were all missing him dearly. His mother would cry often, his father would recite sorrowful poems for him and the children would ask after their brother. So when some of Zayd's family performed Hajj, they decided to look for him in Mecca. They asked around for him in the hope that they might find him and indeed they discovered him at the *masjid*, recognising one another instantly.

The reunion was an emotional one and they wished to hurry him back to his parents. They asked him how he was and where he was living. He told them of his master, Muhammad, and asked them to reassure his parents on his behalf. Surprised that he did not return with them, his father and granduncle hurried to Mecca when they received news of his whereabouts.

When the two men arrived, they asked after Muhammad and found him in the *masjid*. When they met him, they tried their best to compliment him to garner good favour, "O son of Abdul Muttalib, O son of Hashim. You are the people whom Allah has given the Sanctuary, you help its residents and you feed its prisoners. We have come to you regarding our son who is with you. Be gracious to us please! Be kind to us and set him free from a ransom." Muhammad asked them, knowing full well who they spoke of, "Who is he?" They responded, "Zayd ibn Haritha. With the price for freedom you desire." Muhammad thought awhile and replied, "Nothing else?"

The two men were embarrassed and asked, "What else is there? We will give you a ransom that you desire. Or else, kindly grant him freedom." Muhammad said with clarity, "Call him and I will ask him to make his decision. If he chooses to go back with you, then truly he is yours to take. I will not be a barrier between what he chooses and myself." The two men smiled as their faces lit up. "You have granted us fairness," they said.

Muhammad called for Zayd. Zayd shared an emotional reunion with his father and uncle, and as they shed their tears, Muhammad said, "O Zayd. I am the person you know me to be. You have seen my companionship towards you. Choose to stay with me or to depart with them." Zayd's reply baffled his relatives. Addressing Muhammad, he said, "I cannot choose anyone over you. You are both a father and an uncle to me."

Taken aback, the two men felt certain that Zayd's immaturity had clouded his judgment. Choosing to stay enslaved was something akin to madness, so his father said firmly to him,

"What is wrong Zayd, that you would prefer to stay a slave over freedom? Would you prefer this man over your father and uncle? And indeed, over your whole family?" Zayd replied quietly but with conviction, "Yes, I have seen something remarkable in this man. I am not able to choose anyone over him."

With the greatest respect for his guests, Muhammad concluded the discussion. They all then went to the Kaba and stood by the people there in order to certify the agreement that had passed. Muhammad said, "O those present, bare witness that Zayd is my son. I inherit from him and he inherits from me." When Zayd's father and uncle witnessed this spectacle, their hearts became satisfied and they acknowledged that their son had chosen the gateway to honour. And so they departed, leaving Zayd to his adopted father and freedom.

Zayd went on to hold an important position in the spreading of Islam through *dawah* and *jihad*. He soon married Zaynab bint Jahsh and climbed the ranks to become the leader of many victorious battalions, until sadly he died leading his army into battle, when he was martyred at Mu'tah. Allah's Messenger ﷺ wept profusely over Zayd's loss.

His nickname was "the beloved of the Prophet ﷺ", and of all the great Companions, the Quran only mentions Zayd by name. The Prophet used to say, "The most beloved person to me is the one who Allah has blessed and whom I have favoured." That is to say, Allah blessed Zayd ibn al-Haritha with Islam and the Prophet ﷺ favoured him by granting him his freedom.

ALI IBN ABU TALIB

Even after Muhammad ibn Abdullah left his uncle Abu Talib's house, he would still worry for him. Muhammad would often talk about his life in his uncle's house and tell his children fond stories from his time there. He was always keen to return his kindness to him, so when a food crisis hit Mecca and life became quite difficult for the less affluent, he had an idea that might help relieve Abu Talib of his burdens a little. He approached his uncle, Abbas ibn Abdul Muttalib, for help.

Abbas was the richest person amongst Bani Hashim and similar in age to Muhammad. "O Abbas," he said, "Indeed your brother Abu Talib has many children and has been afflicted by this food crisis. Let us go to him so we can see how to alleviate his difficulties. I could take one of his younger children as my ward, you could take an older child and we could take care of them for him." Abbas, who was also fond of his nephews, agreed that it was a good idea, so they went to Abu Talib with their proposal. He said, "Leave Aqil with me, but take anybody else." So Abbas took in Jafar and Muhammad took in Ali, Abu Talib's youngest son.

This event took place before Muhammad's prophethood, when Ali was only eight years old. When Angel Jibril ﷺ came to the Prophet ﷺ with the first revelations, calling people to faith, the Prophet's house did not hesitate in embracing the message of Islam. And so, Ali was the first young person to enter the faith. Not even ten years of age, Ali was a believer just a few hours after the revelations first came down.

Ali continued to stand by his cousin Prophet Muhammad ﷺ throughout his life. The only time he left his side was on the Prophet's orders in the battle of Tabuk, when Ali was left in charge of Medina. In the early days of oppression, when it was time to pray, Ali would go with his cousin to a Meccan valley in order to hide their faith, even from Ali's own father. However, Abu Talib soon realised that his son had become a Muslim when he saw him worshipping in a way that he did not recognise. He asked him, "My son! What religion are you following?" Ali said to him, "O my father. I believe in Allah, in the Messenger of Allah ﷺ. I believe in the message he has brought, I pray with him to Allah and I follow him."

Ali was the first person to pray with the Prophet ﷺ after Khadija and he never bowed to an idol despite the society he was born into. Ali loved Allah's Messenger ﷺ so much. When the Muhajirun (migrants to Medina) and the Ansar (locals who welcomed the Muhajirun into their homes) were paired off as brothers, he made Ali his own brother. As a person with tremendous knowledge and good judgement, the Prophet ﷺ would often delegate to Ali many important matters. The Prophet ﷺ said, "The best judges amongst them is Ali." The *sira* is filled with Ali's virtues and he himself narrated 586 hadiths from Allah's Messenger directly, such was Ali's prominence in the Prophet's life ﷺ.

AISHA BINT ABU BAKR

Aisha bint Abu Bakr was young when she was betrothed to Allah's Messenger ﷺ. She became his wife in her established adulthood, so in the meantime, the Prophet ﷺ catered to all her needs, ensuring she was comfortable, happy and educated. Aisha's younger friends would visit her to play, sing and race. They would often chat amongst themselves and she would share her mother's handmade cloth dolls with them. One day, the Prophet ﷺ found her playing with her dolls, one of which had two cloth wings. He asked, "What is this?" She said confidently, "A horse." He said, "What are those?" She replied, "Two wings." He said, "A horse with wings?"

She replied, "Didn't Prophet Sulaiman ﷺ have winged horses?!" The Messenger ﷺ could only laugh at her quick-wittedness, laughing until his back teeth showed.

Aisha matured quickly in the Prophet's household and, as a result, she seemed older than her age. But, the Prophet ﷺ continually encouraged her to live her young life with vitality and in good health. One day, they went out together on the morning of a battle. Unbothered by the nearing enemy, he jovially challenged her to a race. Aisha happily accepted the challenge and competitively raced towards the finish line. Gleefully, she beat the army general and even the Prophet ﷺ was happy for her. Even as she neared adulthood, they would still compete from time to time. She accompanied the leader another time and she invited him to a new challenge and race. Convinced she would win just as before, she was a little irritated to find that the Messenger ﷺ beat her this time! He teased, "This is for the last time!"

During their marriage, the Prophet ﷺ would still seek to ensure her entertainment. One day some Abyssinians came to the *masjid* in Medina to show the Companions their skills and dexterity in sports and spear work. Their voices reached Aisha's room that faced the *masjid*. Her room had a doorway with a curtain hanging over it. So when the Prophet ﷺ realised how interested she was, he raised the curtain so she could also see properly. She came up behind him, leant on him and joined in the revelry. Such was the Messenger's demeanour with Aisha, one of utmost gentleness. Jabir ibn Abdullah once said, "Allah's Messenger was an easy-going man. If Aisha desired anything, he would follow it."

She was a fine, young mature woman who knew what Allah's Messenger ﷺ loved. She was known to wear perfume he liked to please his senses. On one journey with him, she wore saffron and musk, placing it in her hair so much so that the hot weather caused the perfume to run onto her face, changing her complexion to a golden, even red colour. The Prophet ﷺ was still so impressed by her beauty that he said, "Your colour, O blonde one, is beautiful."

Naturally Aisha was not like her other older co-wives in her views on life, her status with the Messenger ﷺ, her emotions and her pride of appearance. The other wives were often preoccupied in their affairs or focused on excelling in worship, but Aisha would take another path. She would take lawfully what she needed from the world, wearing clothes that would accentuate her youthfulness. She used to like saffron and rose coloured garments and preferred the more luxurious garments made from silk. Um Abdurrahman bint al-Qasim would say, "Whilst she was on pilgrimage, I saw upon Aisha clothes as red as sparks of fire."

Aisha always sought the Prophet's contentment ﷺ, she was pleased when he praised her and disliked it greatly when he turned away from her. She was also the one and only of his wives who had not been married before, so she often felt like his true wife in that sense, who he had not married for political or tribal cohesion. She knew the Prophet ﷺ recognised this, but she wanted to make a point. So one day, she said, "O Messenger, if you went to a valley, how would you compare a tree that had been consumed to a tree that was untouched? Which one would you take your camel to? . . . I am that tree."

They would often tease one another in this way, and Allah's Messenger ﷺ could always tell when Aisha was content or upset. He once told her that when she made an oath by the Lord of Muhammad, he could tell that she was happy. However, if she swore by the Lord of the Kaba, it showed that she was annoyed with him. Aisha, surprised that he had discovered her secret habit, laughingly said to him, "By Allah the only thing you temporarily forsake is your name."

Even the Companions knew how much Muhammad ﷺ loved Aisha. However, if her behaviour fell short, like any partner, he was still quick to highlight it. Once, for instance, Aisha felt jealous about one of the Prophet's other wives, Safiya. So Aisha spitefully remarked, "Safiya is quite short." Angered by her unkindness, Muhammad ﷺ reprimanded her, "Enough Aisha. You have said something that would bring a stench to the whole sea if mixed with it."

Aisha was a forthright and smart woman who remained with the Messenger ﷺ for the rest of his life, pleased by keeping herself near to him. Once, Jibril ﷺ descended and as the Prophet ﷺ retold Aisha what Jibril had said, the Prophet ﷺ added, "O Aisha, Jibril sends you his *salam*." Such was her status in Islam.

After the Prophet ﷺ passed away, Aisha remained as a treasure trove of knowledge for the Companions. They would ask her about *fiqh* and *fatwas*, and were corrected by her when discussing the meaning of hadiths. Her youth meant that she was able to spend the rest of her life implementing the Prophet's Sunnah, by directly referencing examples from his home life and private behaviour. Abu Musa al-Ashari narrated, "The Companions of Allah's Messenger never encountered a complication in a matter except that they would go to Aisha to ask her [about it], and they would find knowledge with her."

Aisha is described by various sources and receives fine praise indeed. Ibn Abdul Barr, for example, described her as being, "most unique for her time, [particularly] in *fiqh*, medicine and poetry." Her nephew, Urwa ibn Zubair, also said, "I never met anyone who knew more about the Quran, about obligatory matters, about the lawful and the prohibited, about poetry, or the lineage of the Arabs more than Aisha."

ABDULLAH IBN JAFAR

Medina was facing troubling times of fear and apprehension. The Prophet Muhammad ﷺ was concerned for the army he had sent to Mu'tah under the leadership of Zayd ibn al-Haritha. The army had been tasked with the military response to the murder of the Prophet's envoy by the leader of Basra. The Muslim army were met with tremendous force from the Byzantines. The battle was fierce and Allah's Messenger ﷺ relayed the outcome of events to the Muslims in Medina. He described the warriors' encounters to them so vividly, it was as if they could see their bravery with their own eyes. He informed them when Zayd ibn al-Haritha was killed, when Jafar ibn Abu Talib was killed and when Abdullah ibn Rawahah was killed. Finally, he gave them news of Khalid ibn al-Walid's newly assumed leadership and how he had ultimately saved the surviving warriors by retreating.

Among the deceased was Jafar, the Prophet's cousin. Historians say that he was born in Abyssinia and was in fact the first Muslim there. He grew up there and later went to Medina with his father. He memorised knowledge from the Messenger ﷺ and also narrated hadiths from him. After his death, Prophet Muhammad ﷺ was very concerned for Jafar's children, now recognised as orphans after their father's martyrdom. He visited Jafar's widow, Asma bint Umais, and when he entered her home he said, "Bring me the children of Jafar." When they arrived, he began to hug them, crying with them and showing them affection for their loss. He then invited them to his own home where they stayed comfortably as guests for three days. In that time, he would also preach to them to reduce their sorrow and prepare them for their new life. Abdullah once narrated, "I stayed three nights in the house of Allah's Messenger. We would follow him every time he moved room. Then we went back home and Allah's Messenger said, 'Do not weep over my brother after today.'"

After a month, the army finally returned from Mu'tah to Medina, and people young and old flocked to greet them. Allah's Messenger rode on his animal to join the welcome, all the while showing kindness to the children in the crowd. He said to his Companions, "Take the [other] children and pass me Jafar's son." Abdullah was brought to him and Muhammad ﷺ placed him on the front of his mount. Whilst the other children were reuniting with their families, he knew how much this son in particular would want to see his father on that day. Not wanting Abdullah to feel the loss of his father more keenly and get lost in the crowd, Allah's Messenger ﷺ kept him close and consoled him for the loss of his father. The Prophet ﷺ stroked his head tenderly and prayed for him saying, "O Allah bless Jafar's offspring and bless Abdullah in his transactions. I am their guardian in this world and in the Hereafter."

The Prophet ﷺ continued to keep an eye on Jafar's children, caring for them as much as he could. If he passed Abdullah on the streets, he would carry him on his mount just as before, treating him with honour and kindness. Allah's Messenger ﷺ also thought that Abdullah looked like him and would say, "[He] resembles me in my features and my behaviour," so the young boy was raised on the prophetic model of behaviour and started to work in trade at a young age, just as Muhammad ﷺ had done. He would head to the market and do as merchants do. When the Prophet ﷺ passed him there, he would say, "O Allah bless him in his transactions."

Whenever the children of Medina learned that the Prophet ﷺ was on the verge of entering the city, Abdullah would race past all the other children to greet the Prophet ﷺ. When the Messenger ﷺ saw him, he would carry him and one of Fatima's sons on his mount into the city. They would enter Medina smiling radiantly, and so this orphan child found a new type of belonging with the beloved Prophet ﷺ.

ABDULLAH IBN ABBAS

Abdullah ibn Abbas was born during a very difficult time for the Muslim community. His mother gave birth to him whilst the Banu Hashim were living in exile. The Quraysh were preventing their access to food and attacking them both socially and economically without relent so as to secure their surrender. But Allah foiled their plans, and Islam soon spread steadily across the region.

And so, Abdullah ibn Abbas eventually grew up in safety, influenced by the graceful conduct and knowledge of the Prophet ﷺ. He loved Abdullah and all of Abbas' children dearly. He would play with them all, often lining them up for races towards him. The little ones would be so passionate, and everyone wanted to beat one another. They'd race hard and when they would reach the Prophet ﷺ at the end line, they would climb onto his chest and back, and he would receive them with joy and affection.

Ibn Abbas, as he came to be known, was very sharp and alert. Although he was young, he received a lot of benefit from his nearness to al-Mustafa. One night, whilst staying at his Aunt Maimuna's home, he saw the Prophet ﷺ performing *wudu* lightly from a jug and turning to pray. Following in his footsteps closely, Abdullah also performed his *wudu* and went to stand near the Prophet ﷺ. Muhammad ﷺ moved Abdullah to his right-hand side so that Abdullah could learn how to be led in prayer.

Abdullah suddenly felt embarrassed, so when the Prophet ﷺ asked him what was wrong, Abdullah said meekly, "O Messenger of Allah, it doesn't suit you that anyone should pray beside you when you are the Messenger of Allah." Muhammad ﷺ was surprised, he stroked young Abdullah's head and turned in supplication saying, "O Allah, teach him wisdom and the explanation of the Book. O Allah, bless him therein, spread [the *deen*] from him and make him of your righteous servants. O Allah, grant him a deep understanding of the religion." The young boy was overwhelmed that the Prophet ﷺ himself had prayed for him personally and exclaimed, "The Prophet asked Allah to give me wisdom on two occasions!"

Another time, the Prophet ﷺ was riding a camel with him and Abdullah wanted to make use of his time with him, so he asked the Prophet ﷺ to teach him a hadith of great benefit. Muhammad ﷺ advised him,

Be mindful of Allah and Allah will protect you. Be mindful of Allah and you will find Allah before you. If you ask someone, ask Allah. If you seek help, seek Allah's help. Know well, that if the people were to come together to provide you some benefit, they would not benefit you except with what is written for you. If they all gathered to harm you with something, they could only harm you with something that has been written for you. The pens have been lifted and the scrolls have dried.

The Prophet Muhammad ﷺ and Abdullah had a close relationship throughout their lives. Abdullah narrates that once, when he visited his Aunt Maimuna with the Prophet ﷺ and Khalid ibn al-Walid, "She came to us with a bowl of milk. The Prophet drank from it. I was on his right and Khalid was on his left. The Prophet said to me, 'It is for you to drink, but if you wish I will give preference to Khalid.' I said, 'O Messenger of Allah. I couldn't prefer anyone else [but myself] for your leftover water!' "

The Prophet ﷺ let Abdullah drink first and then taught him that, "Whoever is fed by Allah should say, 'Allah bless us in this food, and feed us with what is better than this.' And if Allah gives him milk to drink, he should say, '. . . and increase us in it,' as no food or drink benefits us like milk."

The Prophet's call to Islam influenced Abdullah so much so that he himself excelled in acquiring knowledge. He memorised a large number of hadiths at a young age directly from the Prophet ﷺ and continued to learn prophetic sayings from senior Companions until he finally memorised a total of 1,660 hadiths. He had one of the best memories for hadiths amongst the Companions and soon came to be known as "*habr al-ummah*" (scholar of the ummah). Ibn Abbas also worked considerably hard to learn the Quran personally from the Prophet ﷺ. He said of himself, "When the Prophet died, I had already learned *al-Muffasal al-Muhkam*(from surah forty-nine to the end of the Quran).

As Ibn Abbas grew older, he was held in high esteem amongst his people because of his knowledge and virtues. He was known as *tarjuman al-Quran* (the interpreter of the Quran), and would interpret it for whoever asked. It was said that, "If you saw [Abdullah] you would say that he is the most handsome of people. When he spoke, you would say that he is the most eloquent of people." Such was Abdullah's wisdom, that even the great Umar ibn al-Khattab would refer to him on the most complex of issues. When Umar was challenged by such a problem, he would invite Abdullah along with some of the most eminent Companions, and seat Abdullah nearest to him to recognise his status. Umar was asked, "How can you include him with the elders, while he is still a young man?" He would reply, "He has a questioning tongue and an intelligent heart."

Ibn Abbas was well versed in the lawful and the prohibited, in Arabic, in genealogy and in poetry. It was said that, "Nobody knew the Sunnah, nor were they superior in opinions, nor sharper in analysis than him." His companions called him the sea and the scholar of the ummah, such was the legacy of Abdullah Ibn Abbas, a child who grew up around the Prophet ﷺ.

UMAMA BINT HAMZA

Hamza ibn Abdul Muttalib was the dearest uncle of the Prophet ﷺ. He contributed in many ways to the Prophet's cause and came to be known as "The Leader of the Martyrs" after he was martyred in the Battle of Uhud. He left behind him a daughter, Umama, who went to live with her mother in Mecca after his death.

A few years later, when he was performing Umrah in the year 7 AH, Umama saw Allah's Messenger and called upon him, "My uncle, My uncle!" Ali was concerned for Umama, and so he picked her up and passed her onto Fatima's camel. The Prophet ﷺ said to Fatima, "Before you, Fatima, is your uncle's daughter. Carry her!" When it was agreed by all that it would be better for Umama to come back with them to Medina, the Companions began quarrelling over who would be her guardian. Ali and Jafar, the sons of Abu Talib, and Zayd ibn al-Haritha all wanted to look after her in honour of her late father, Hamza.

The Prophet Muhammad ﷺ said, "Come here. I shall decide between you all." Ali had thought to bring her to Medina, and so he said, "Umama is my uncle's daughter and I am married to the Messenger of Allah's daughter, so she has more right over her." Jafar said, "She is my uncle's daughter, and my wife, Asma bint Umais, is her maternal aunt, so she has more right over her."

The Prophet ﷺ had joined Hamza and Zayd as brothers after the hijra, so Zayd said, "She is my brother Hamza's daughter, so I have more right over her."

After the Prophet ﷺ listened to them all, he judged in favour of Jafar because of Umama's relationship with her aunt. He said, "The maternal aunt is akin to a mother. [Also] a woman cannot marry her paternal or maternal aunt's husband," so Umamah would have been best suited to Jafar's household. Praising all three Companions for their attempts to care for the girl, he first turned to Ali saying, "You are from me and I am from you." He then said to Jafar, "You resemble me most in your features and manners." And finally, he said to Zayd, "You are our brother and freed from bondship."

Umama remained with Jafar until he was martyred in the battle of Mu'tah. Allah's Messenger ﷺ then put her in Ali's care. She stayed as his ward until she became a young woman, then Ali suggested that the Prophet ﷺ consider marrying her. The Prophet however declined immediately and said, "She is my suckling brother's daughter," because Hamza and Muhammad ﷺ had been suckled together. Instead, the Prophet ﷺ married Umama to his stepson, Salama.

USAMA IBN ZAYD

As Zayd ibn al-Haritha's son, Usama ibn Zayd was very beloved to Allah's Messenger ﷺ. Just like his father before him, the Prophet ﷺ treated Usama like a family member and he too became part of the household. Born and raised in Mecca, Usama soon came to be known as the "beloved son of the Beloved". When asked about his most loved children, the Prophet ﷺ said, "The most beloved of people to me besides Fatima is Usama, but none besides him." He also said, "Usama is the most beloved of people to me. My hope is that he will be of the righteous, so I counsel you to treat him well." The Prophet ﷺ held Usama in such high esteem that he once remarked, "Whoever loves Allah and the Messenger must love Usama."

Usama's mother was Umm Ayman, an Abyssinian woman who was a freed slave of the Prophet ﷺ. She stayed with him after his mother died and had served him loyally. He said of her, "Whoever would like to marry a woman from the people of Paradise, he should marry Umm Ayman," so his adopted son and previously freed slave himself, Zayd ibn al-Haritha, married her. After Umm Ayman and Zayd had baby Usama, the Prophet ﷺ would say of him, "He is what remains of my household."

Usama grew up under the Prophet's influence at a time when the revelation was fresh and Islam was still growing. The Prophet ﷺ was still subject to much persecution, but this opened Usama's eyes to the state of the world and brought the two closer. Muhammad ﷺ cared for Usama much in the same way that he cared for his grandsons, Hasan and Hussain. He would put Usama on one thigh and Hasan with Hussain on the other, hug them all and say, "Allah, have mercy on them, for I show mercy to them. O Allah, love them, for I show love to them."

After his father Zayd was martyred at the battle of Mu'tah, young Usama and the Prophet ﷺ only became closer. Such was the Prophet's regard for Usama that on his farewell pilgrimage, Muhammad ﷺ delayed his descent into Muzdalifa just to wait for Usama's arrival. Usama was not very handsome or impressive to behold, so when he arrived the Yemeni people amongst the pilgrims remarked, "For *him* were we held back?" But appearances of course did not matter to the Prophet ﷺ, and they departed for Mecca together.

As Usama grew older, he grew wiser and was keen to be a high achiever, so the Messenger ﷺ sent him to defend the territories of Islam. He closely supervised Usama's development and nurtured his enthusiasm. Usama, however, did make mistakes and the Prophet ﷺ, although forgiving, would not hesitate to teach him right from wrong. For instance, on one occasion it reached Muhammad ﷺ that Usama had encountered an enemy in battle. As Usama raised his spear to defeat him, the man said, "There is no God but Allah," hoping to be saved from death. Usama presumed that the man was being deceitful and was simply trying to save himself, so he drove his spear through him regardless.

The Messenger ﷺ was appalled by what Usama had done and, despite his love for him, he reprimanded him severely, "Woe to you Usama! What are you going to do with 'There is no God but Allah? There is no God but Allah?' " The Prophet ﷺ continued to repeat that phrase until Usama was rendered speechless and filled with remorse. It was not for him to presume the man's deceit.

Despite this and other mistakes, the Prophet ﷺ did not lose love for Usama. When Muhammad ﷺ fell sick before his death, Usama was about eighteen years old and on the cusp of manhood. Confident in his competence and bravery, the Prophet ﷺ appointed Usama as an army commander. He tasked him with going to Mu'tah, where his father Zayd had died, to avenge his father and seek justice. Some of the Companions were concerned, however, that Usama was still too young and that he would not be skilled enough to complete such an important mission. They said, "A youngster? Whilst the Muhajirun and Ansar remain?"

Their words angered the Prophet ﷺ considerably and although he was critically ill, he climbed the *minbar* and said, "O People! What are these words that have reached me from some of you about my appointment of Usama? If you are critical of my appointment, then it implies you were critical of his father's appointment before him. I swear by Allah he was most suitable to be a commander, and his son too is most appropriate as a leader after him. They are proper for all good tasks, so treat him well because he is of the best of you."

Even as the Prophet's illness became worse, he used to repeat, "Dispatch Usama's troops." Usama finally departed for Mu'tah, and he was only camped outside Medina when news of the Prophet's passing came. He returned immediately to Medina to mourn the beloved Messenger's loss ﷺ.

After Abu Bakr took command, one of his first orders was to dispatch Usama to Mu'tah as the Prophet ﷺ had wished. There, Usama fulfilled the Messenger's command by successfully invading Byzantine territory and opening up the path for the later Levantine conquest. The Companions continued to hold Usama in high esteem because of his closeness to the Prophet ﷺ. Umar ibn Al-Khattab even allocated him a stipend that was worth more than double of his own son's. His son, Abdullah, made mention of this to his father, "You have given more to Usama than me, although I attended battles he did not?" Umar explained, "Indeed, Usama was dearer to the Prophet than you. His father was also dearer to the Prophet than your own father."

THE PROPHET'S ﷺ CHILDREN

The Prophet Muhammad ﷺ fathered three sons and four daughters. All children, apart from Ibrahim (who he had with Maria), were born to his first wife, Khadija. In chronological order, his children were:

- Qasim
- Zainab
- Ruqayyah
- Umm Kulthum
- Abdullah
- Fatima
- Ibrahim

THE PROPHET'S SONS: QASIM, ABDULLAH AND IBRAHIM

All three of the Prophet's ﷺ sons died tragically in their infancy. His very first child was Qasim, who earned Muhammad ﷺ the nickname "Abu al-Qasim", but sadly Qasim died before his second birthday. After some time, he had another son with Khadija called Abdullah, who was affectionately nicknamed Tayyib or Tahir. Little is known about his first two sons, but we do know that baby Abdullah died before he was even weaned. We do know a little more about the loss of his last son, Ibrahim, and the story of his mother, Maria.

In the seventh year after the Hijra, Hatib ibn Abu Balta arrived in Medina on his return from Egypt. With him, he brought a gift of two servants from Muqawqis, the Governor of Alexandria, for the Prophet ﷺ. The two maidservants, Mariya and Sirin, found in their new master a kind man. Muhammad ﷺ wed Sirin to his poet and Companion,

Hassan ibn Thabit, and then married Mariya himself. The Prophet ﷺ showed Mariya immense compassion and was particularly sensitive to the fact that she was so far from home. He made a comfortable house for Mariya in a Medinan palm field and would visit her there regularly. They soon had the happy news of a child, and when she gave birth to a young boy, they named him Ibrahim, after his forefather.

Ibrahim was born in the outskirts of Medina at his mother's home. Salma, a freed slave of the Prophet ﷺ (who was now Abu Rafi's wife), hurried to the Messenger to give him the good news of his son's birth. He was so overjoyed that he rewarded her with a servant to join her household. On the seventh day after his birth, the Prophet ﷺ shaved Ibrahim's hair off, donated its weight in silver to charity, buried his hair and gave him his blessed name. Allah's Messenger ﷺ would visit his son Ibrahim every day to pour love and affection on him. Muhammad ﷺ would hold him, kiss him and enjoy the smell of his newborn skin. Anas ibn Malik once said, "Ibrahim was suckling in the outskirts of Medina, and so the Prophet would take us with him. We would go in and he would pick him up, kiss him and return."

But his perfect happiness with Ibrahim did not last even a year and a half before his beloved son was taken from this world. The Prophet ﷺ took Abdul Rahman ibn Awf's hand and, filled with sorrow, he entered the room where Ibrahim lay dying in his mother's lap. He said, "O Ibrahim. We cannot avail you from Allah at all." When his soul left his body, the Prophet's eyes shed quiet tears until Abdul Rahman felt heartbroken at the sight. He asked him, "Do you weep, although you have asked us not to?" Although the Prophet ﷺ was in the heavy throes of grief, he replied,

> O ibn Awf, I did not prohibit you from weeping. I prohibited you from two ridiculous noises: the sound of a stringed instrument playing the pipes of Shaytan and the sound of smacking one's own face and tearing one's clothes in the event of a tragedy. . . As for this, this is kindness and one who is not kind, will not be shown kindness. If it wasn't for His true word and His true promise [that the last of us will meet the first of us] we would have wept over this even more severely. Indeed, Ibrahim we are grieved. The eyes weep, but we do not say what Allah dislikes.

Mariya was also, of course, weeping for her child, but the Prophet ﷺ gently reminded her not to wail. He then commanded that his child be bathed and shrouded. Fadl ibn Abbas did this for the Prophet ﷺ and Muhammad then said to them, "Do not place his shroud down until I have seen him." When Ibrahim was ready, the Prophet ﷺ came to see him and his tears began to flow again. They carried Ibrahim to the Baqi cemetery in Medina. The Prophet ﷺ prayed for him a total of four times there. He was sat on the edge of the grave when Fadl descended into it with Usamah ibn Zayd (and Ali too, it is reported) to complete the burial with the Prophet ﷺ. Once it was done, Muhammad ﷺ said, "Peace be upon you" and he commanded that water should be sprayed from a jug over the grave and placed a distinguishing marker on it.

That day, a solar eclipse filled the sky. Some of the Companions wondered whether it had happened because of the death of Ibrahim. Disappointed by this, the Prophet ﷺ led six *rakat* of prolonged prayer with them, then said, "O people, indeed the sun and the moon are from the signs of Allah. Eclipses do not happen because someone dies or is born. If you witness an eclipse, then pray. Then continue praying until the eclipse is over." Even on the day of his son's burial, he took the opportunity to spread Allah's wisdom.

The Prophet's care and compassion for Mariya continued. He showered her with love until the end of his days, treating her with the honour and goodness she deserved. Ibrahim's death meant that the Prophet ﷺ did not have a male descendant, after having also lost Qasim and Abdullah in the years before. And so Allah said in the Quran, "Muhammad is not a father of any of your men. But he is Allah's Messenger and Seal of the Prophets. Allah has knowledge over all things." (33:40)

When Muhammad ﷺ was still living in Mecca, the polytheists cruelly rejoiced that his sons Qasim and Abdullah had died. They said, "Muhammad has no offspring. His lineage and descendants have come to an end. He is impotent and his lineage will be cut-off after his demise." But Allah revealed to him, "Indeed, I have given you al-Kawthar. Pray to your Lord and sacrifice. Those who ridicule you are cut-off" (Quran 109:1-3).

THE PROPHET'S 🌸 DAUGHTERS

ZAYNAB

Zaynab was Muhammad's 🌸 first child from his first love, Khadija bint Khuwaylid. Zaynab was born ten years before the Prophet 🌸 received the first revelation. As the daughter of such excellent and noble parents, Zaynab was a model of virtue and honour and grew up in a household filled with harmony and love.

When Zaynab was old enough for marriage, her cousin Abu al-As ibn al-Rabia asked for her hand in marriage. He descended from Abdul Manaf ibn Qusay, the Prophet's grandfather, and from the maternal side, he descended from Khuwaylid, Khadija's father. Despite his young age, he was one of the leading merchants of the Quraysh. His wisdom and good character commanded the respect of the people and their elders.

Abu al-As was very close to his aunt Khadija, who treated him like her own son. He often visited his aunt's house and every time he saw Zaynab, he was taken by her beauty, gentleness and good nature. Zaynab was also at ease in his presence and loved to listen to his speeches and his jokes. Naturally, their two hearts opened to one another.

When Abu al-As asked for Zaynab's hand in marriage, Prophet Muhammad 🌸 received him well and listened to him attentively but said he would ask his daughter's opinion. He 🌸 went to Zaynab and told her, "Daughter, your cousin, Abu al-As ibn al-Rabia, is interested in you." Zaynab kept quiet out of shyness and she did not utter a word. But her face became red and she shut her eyes. The Messenger of Allah 🌸 smiled and did not repeat the question, for he understood what was in her heart. He then went back to Abu al-As, shook his hand in congratulations and made a supplication to bless their union.

Zaynab and Abu al-As had a tumultuous but ultimately great love story. They happily had two children, a son called Ali and a daughter called Umama, who were the Prophet's first grandchildren. But, when the Messenger ﷺ received his call to Islam, this divided the couple's loyalties, and the couple reluctantly parted ways for a number of years. Towards the end of Zaynab's life, Abu al-As finally saw the beauty of Islam and renewed his marriage with his beloved wife. But their happy reunion was to be short-lived. Zaynab, who had been suffering from haemorrhage complications since a fall in her first attempted migration to Medina, sadly died a year later, in the fifth year after the Hijra.

When the Prophet ﷺ came to bid farewell to his daughter. His eyes were full of tears and his heart full of sorrow. The grief held a double sting for him as Zaynab's death reminded him of the death of her mother, his darling wife Khadija. The Prophet ﷺ said to the women performing the ritual bathing of Zaynab, "Wash her three times and let the last wash be mixed with camphor oil." After they washed her, he prayed over his beloved daughter's body. May Allah be pleased with Zaynab, the first child of the Messenger of Allah ﷺ.

RUQAYYA

When Ruqayya was born three years after Zaynab, she was a huge source of happiness to her parents, Prophet Muhammad ﷺ and Khadija, who lavished her with love. And they were soon to be blessed with further joy through a third daughter, Umm Kulthum. At a time when baby girls were undesired and even buried alive for their gender, it is even more poignant how much the Prophet ﷺ and Khadija cherished and loved their daughters, whom they saw as nothing less than miraculous gifts from Allah.

Ruqayya and Umm Kulthum were so close in age that they were brought up together like they were twin sisters. Both were married to their cousin brothers, but these marriages were divorced before they were even consummated. Abu Lahab and Umm Jamil were both the girls' uncles and fathers-in-law. But both had forced their sons to divorce Ruqayya and Umm Kulthum on news of their nephew, Muhammad's, newly acquired prophethood.

Ruqayya bore this hardship patiently along with her father. After being dishonoured by Abu Lahab's son when he divorced her, she was in fact destined to marry one of the best of men, Uthman ibn Affan ibn Abi al-As. Uthman was one of the first eight people to enter Islam and one of the ten who were informed that they would enter Paradise. He was later to become one of the Rightly Guided Caliphs.

When the Prophet ﷺ permitted his Companions to leave for Abyssinia, the newlyweds, Uthman and Ruqayya, were among the emigrants. Ruqayya hugged her father, mother and sisters, almost choking with sorrow and distress at having to part with them. After reaching Abyssinia, Ruqayya and Uthman lived in peace, but eventually they returned to Mecca only to discover the situation had worsened for the Muslims there.

Ruqayya was about to face another personal and tragic blow. When she entered her father's house, she learned that her beloved mother, Khadija, had died. Ruqayya could not stop weeping, but she accepted Allah's decree, and placed her trust and fate entirely in His hands. Uthman and Ruqayya did not stay long in Mecca. They migrated to Medina once the Ansar – the Aws and Khazraj tribes – had pledged allegiance to Muhammad ﷺ. As such, Ruqayya became known as the "lady of two emigrations."

In Medina, Ruqayya gave birth to her only child, who they named Abdullah. After enduring years of hardship, Ruqayya and Uthman's son filled his parents' lives with happiness. But they were to be tested, yet again. One day, while Abdullah was sleeping in his cradle, a rooster appeared and pecked at his eyes. This led to an infection that claimed his life a few days later. Ruqayya's heart was broken in two, and she contracted a terrible fever. Her loving husband stayed by the side of his wife nursing her and begging Allah to alleviate her suffering and make her recover from her illness. While he was nursing his sick wife, he heard the voice of the announcer calling on the emigrants and the Ansar to help accost the caravan of the Quraysh that was on its way back from Syria. Uthman felt he must go and do his duty, but the Prophet ﷺ commanded him to remain close to his sick wife to care for her until she recovered.

But Ruqayya was never to recover. Her disease was so severe that it claimed her life. At the same time that the bereaved Uthman kissed his wife's forehead and fingertips, proclamations could be heard outside announcing the Muslims' victory. The Messenger of Allah ﷺ was distraught to hear the news of his daughter's death. He moved closer to her side and sorrowfully bade her farewell. Fatima, the Prophet's youngest daughter, stood by Ruqayya's deathbed weeping for her dear sister. The Prophet ﷺ helped her to her feet and gently wiped her tears away with his garment. The bereaved father ﷺ performed the funeral prayers for his daughter and followed her body to the place of burial. And so ended the life of the patient and pious Ruqayya.

UMM KULTHUM

Umm Kulthum was born shortly after Ruqayya and became an excellent companion to her sister. As stated before, they were raised like twins. When Ruqayya married Uthman and emigrated to Abyssinia with him, Umm Kulthum and their younger sister Fatima stayed in Mecca to witness the severest period of persecution against her father and the early Muslims. Umm Kulthum, taking the mantle of the eldest daughter, tried her best to help in the household affairs and to relieve the Prophet's grief at the cruel rejection of the Meccan pagans. Things were about to become even worse. The people of the Quraysh decided to strike an economic and social boycott against the Muslims and Banu Hashim. Umm Kulthum, along with her family and the early band of Muslims, were driven out of their homes to mete out a life in the valley of Abu Talib. Here, exposed to the harsh environment, they suffered starvation, isolation and extreme hardship for years. Umm Kulthum endured the afflictions of the siege and the pains of hunger side by side with her father and the Muslim community.

They survived on leaves and even dirt. Umm Kulthum cared as well as she could for her father, her younger sister and her mother, who was very ill and weak. Finally, after three long years, the oppressive boycott ended. But it took its toll on the noble Khadija. Her disease grew fatal and she tragically died, leaving her family heartbroken. Umm Kulthum then shouldered the responsibility of managing the Prophet's household affairs.

After the Hijra to Medina, Umm Kulthum finally enjoyed a life of peace and contentment. Her dear sister Ruqayya also returned to the family and lived in happiness in Medina, witnessing her father gain victory against the oppressive Quraysh. After having to endure terrible suffering during the boycott, Umm Kulthum's heart lifted in joy to see the return of her father victorious from the Battle of Badr.

But soon after that, Ruqayya, her beloved twin-like sister, suddenly died. Three years passed and Umm Kulthum's heart was still shadowed in sorrow for the loss of her sister. She saw how Ruqayya's grieving husband, Uthman, would often come to her father to receive condolence, advice and support over the death of his precious wife. She saw how the tears rolled down his cheeks in grief. One day, Umar ibn al-Khattab came complaining to the Prophet ﷺ that both Abu Bakr and Uthman refused his offer to marry his daughter Hafsa. The Prophet ﷺ said to him, "Hafsa will marry someone who is better than Uthman, and Uthman will marry someone better than Hafsa." Then the Prophet ﷺ addressed Uthman saying, "I am giving you Umm Kulthum, Ruqayya's sister, in marriage. If I had ten daughters, I would have married them to you in succession." And so Umm Kulthum married the noble Uthman and he earned the title "The Possessor of the Two Lights" because he had been married to two cherished daughters of the blessed Prophet Muhammad ﷺ.

Umm Kulthum lived happily with Uthman for the next six years. In later years, after the conquest of Mecca in the year 8 AH, Umm Kulthum yearned to visit the grave of her mother, Khadija. But Umm Kulthum never managed to pray over her mother's grave again, as she passed away soon afterwards. The Messenger of Allah ﷺ buried her beside the remains of her beloved sister, Ruqayya. As in life, these two sisters were brought together in death, buried side by side. May Allah be pleased with the 'twin' sisters and beloved daughters of the Prophet ﷺ.

FATIMA AL-ZAHRA

Fatima al-Zahra bint Muhammad was an individual of extraordinary and excellent character. She was strong, courageous and utterly devoted to Allah. She had a very special and beautiful bond with her father, Allah's messenger ﷺ. Fatima was the fourth daughter of the Prophet ﷺ and Khadija. She was born at the time when her noble father had begun to seek out solitude in the mountains around Mecca, where he would meditate on the great mysteries of creation.

Fatima watched as her older sisters, who pampered and looked after her, got married and left the family home. A cloud of sadness passed over the little girl. Fatima was inconsolable and her mother tenderly asked her why she wept so much. Fatima said, "Do not allow anybody to take me away from you and my father. I cannot bear to leave you!" Her mother then smiled lovingly at her daughter and said gently, "You will never leave us, except if you wish to."

Young Fatima found some comfort in the friendship she had with Ali, her father's cousin, who was only two years older than her and lived with them in the Prophet's house. Yet when Fatima was five years old, a great event was about to occur that would change everything - her father was appointed as God's messenger to all of humanity. Her mother, Khadija, carefully explained to her young daughter what the Prophet ﷺ had to do. Fatima was an unusually sensitive child for her age. She drew even closer to her father ﷺ and grew in wisdom, loyalty and resilience alongside her father's mission. As a child, she would often be found walking courageously by his side through the narrow streets and alleys of Mecca, attending secret gatherings of the early Muslims who had pledged allegiance to the Prophet ﷺ or visiting the Holy Sanctuary.

One day, when she was not yet ten, she accompanied her father to the Kaba. As he stood facing the holy precinct to pray, Fatima did not leave his side. A group from the Quraysh began to gather around him. Among them were the prominent pagan leaders Abu Jahl ibn Hisham, Uqbah ibn Abi Muayt, Umayyah ibn Khalaf, Shaybah and Utbah. With cruel intent, the group moved closer to the Prophet ﷺ and Abu Jahl, the ringleader, sneered, "Which of you can bring the entrails of a slaughtered animal and throw it on Muhammad?"

Uqbah ibn Abi Muayt was only too eager, and scurried off, returning with the filthy entrails and threw them on the blessed shoulders of the Prophet ﷺ while he was still prostrating. One of the Prophet's own companions, Abdullah ibn Masud, was fearful of the mighty Quraysh leaders and powerless to do or say anything. But Fatima was enraged to see her father being so humiliated. This young girl, still only nine years old, promptly went to her father and removed the offensive matter with her own hands. She then turned, stood firm and angrily rebuked the Qurayshi men. Astonished at her fearlessness, they did not speak a single word to her. When the Quraysh used to mock the Prophet ﷺ, they would say, "Muhammad has only daughters." Now they saw what a tower of strength his daughter could be.

On another occasion, Fatima was with the Prophet ﷺ as he made *tawaf* (circumambulation) around the Kaba. A Quraysh mob gathered around him, seized him and tried to strangle him with his own clothes. Fatima screamed and shouted for help. Abu Bakr heard her cries and came rushing to the scene and managed to free the Prophet ﷺ. While he was doing so, he pleaded, "Would you kill a man who says, 'My Lord is God?' " But the mob turned on Abu Bakr and began beating him until blood came flowing from his head and face. Thus was Fatima exposed to witnessing such violence and cruelty against her beloved father and the early Muslims. She did not retreat in fear or shyness but fought against the injustice like a true warrior.

Fatima's young life continued to be shaped with trials and challenges. She was one of the youngest members of the clans at about twelve years old, when she suffered hunger and thirst along with her family in the valley of Abu Talib during the boycott. Three years later when it was lifted, Fatima was about to face the tragic loss of one of her parents. Fatima wept bitterly when her wonderful, caring mother Khadija passed away. Fatima was so heartbroken that her health deteriorated, some even feared she might die of grief.

However, Fatima knew she had to become even more resilient for her father, the noble Prophet ﷺ. She devoted herself to his care, giving him comfort and solace during every difficult moment. Fatima was so concerned for the Prophet's ﷺ welfare that she came to be called "Umm Abiha", the mother of her father.

The Prophet ﷺ had a deep and special bond with his beloved Fatima. He once said, "Whoever pleased Fatima has indeed pleased God and whoever has caused her to be angry has indeed angered God. Fatima is a part of me. Whatever pleases her pleases me and whatever angers her angers me." The Prophet's love and esteem for his daughter can be truly felt in his following words, "The best women in all the world are four: the Virgin Mary, Asiya - the wife of Pharoah, Khadija - Mother of the Believers, and Fatima - daughter of Muhammad." Fatima thus took a unique place in the Prophet's heart that was only otherwise occupied by his wife Khadija.

When the situation became worse than ever for the Muslims in Mecca, the Prophet ﷺ decreed that the emigration begin to Medina. Fatima was then eighteen years old. Many of the great Companions asked for her hand in marriage, such as Abu Bakr and Umar, but the

Prophet ﷺ graciously declined them. Then Ali ibn Abu Talib managed to gather up some courage and went to the Prophet ﷺ to ask for Fatima's hand. Feeling too humble and shy in the presence of the Prophet ﷺ, Ali became tongue-tied. Ali was poor and overcome with nerves, he feared his proposal would be rejected.

The Messenger of Allah ﷺ looked at him with a smiling face and then asked, "What is the matter, son of Abu Talib?" Ali still could not speak and then the Prophet ﷺ gently said, "Perhaps you have come to propose marriage to Fatima?" Ali replied in a very low voice and with an extreme shyness, "Yes. I am asking for the hand of Fatima, daughter of Allah's Messenger in marriage." The Prophet ﷺ responded, "Welcome!" Ali could hardly believe his ears. He took his leave with a happy heart. The Prophet ﷺ then went in to tell his daughter that Ali had come forward to ask for her hand in marriage. Fatima shyly and silently accepted.

And so Fatima was to marry her friend, her relative and one of the dearest men to her father's heart. A year after they married, they were blessed with a baby boy – the Prophet's ﷺ first grandson. He was overjoyed. He recited the adhan in his tiny ear and named him al-Hasan, the beautiful one. The following year, Fatima and Ali were blessed with another son and called him al-Husayn, which means little Hasan or the little beautiful one. The Prophet ﷺ adored his grandsons. Fatima brought them to see the Prophet ﷺ as often as she could, knowing how fond he was of them. Their doting grandfather would take them to the mosque and when he prayed, they would playfully climb onto his back while he prostrated.

In the fifth year after the Hijra, Fatima and Ali were blessed yet again, this time with a daughter whom the Prophet ﷺ named Zaynab. Two years later, Fatima gave birth to a daughter whom the Prophet called Umm Kulthum. He had lovingly named both his granddaughters in memory of their aunts, Fatima's sisters, who had passed away. And so the family of the Messenger of Allah ﷺ extended further through Fatima and Ali's children.

The bond between Fatima and her father only grew stronger throughout her life. The love, the closeness, even Fatima's manner and character were a mirror of the Prophet ﷺ. Aisha, the Mother of the Believers, said of her, "I have not seen anyone of God's creation resemble the Messenger of God more in speech, conversation and manner of sitting than Fatima, may God be pleased with her. When the Prophet saw her approaching, he would welcome her, stand up and kiss her, take her by the hand and sit her down in the place where he was sitting."

Fatima would also do the same when the Prophet ﷺ visited her. She would stand up, joyously welcome him and kiss him. Whenever the Prophet ﷺ returned from a journey, he would pray two *rakahs* (units of prayer) in the mosque and then go to see Fatima before visiting any of his wives.

Fatima lived through trials and sorrows, joys and triumphs alongside the Prophet ﷺ. She had endured the bereavements of her mother Khadija, and her sisters Ruqayya, Zaynab and Umm Kulthum, one after the other. And indeed, Fatima was to be one of the only children of the Prophet to survive him. But now, she was finally struck with the greatest loss of them all, of her dear father, the light of her heart. After the Prophet ﷺ performed his Farewell Pilgrimage, he became seriously ill. Fatima went to visit him at Aisha's home. He welcomed her with a cheerful face and then whispered in her ear, and she wept intensely. Then he ﷺ whispered again in her ear and she laughed.

When the Prophet ﷺ died, Fatima was grief-stricken and tears rolled down her bright cheeks.

Sometime after his death, Aisha asked Fatima once, "Would you please tell me what the Prophet ﷺ whispered to you?" Fatima said,

> As for the first time he whispered to me, he ﷺ said, "Jibril used to review the Glorious Quran with me once a year, but this year, he reviewed it twice. Thus, I think that I am about to die. You should fear Allah and be patient. I am your best predecessor." Accordingly, I wept. But when he noticed my sorrow, he whispered, "Fatima, would you like to be the guardian of the women in Paradise? You will be the first of my family to die after me." Then, I smiled.

Only months after the Prophet ﷺ had passed away, Fatima fell very ill from the grief of separation from her beloved father. One morning, early in the month of Ramadan, Fatima woke up with a look of happiness on her face. She called for Salma bint Umays, who was looking after her, to prepare a bath. She then put on new clothes and perfumed herself and asked Salma to put her bed in the courtyard of the house. She then asked for her husband Ali, who was taken aback when he saw her lying with her face turned towards the sky. He asked her what was wrong, but she smiled and said, "I have an appointment today with the Messenger of God."

Ali wept at the side of his beloved wife as she tried to console him. She bid him look after their children and advised that she should be buried without ceremony. She gazed upwards again, then closed her eyes and surrendered her soul. Fatima al-Zahra had died soon after her father, thus fulfilling the Prophet's prophecy. She was only twenty-seven years old but had experienced so much in her lifetime.

THE PROPHET'S 🌸 GRANDCHILDREN

ALI'S SONS: HASAN AND HUSSAIN

Hasan

Let us consider the lives of the Prophet's 🌸 grandsons more closely. In the third year after the Hijra, the Prophet's grandson, Hasan, was born to Ali and Fatima 🌸 in the Prophet's household. Muhammad 🌸 said of Hasan, "Show me my son!" They raised him up and he gazed at him with love. He asked his parents with interest, "What have you named him?" Ali wanted great things for his son, he wanted him to fight bravely for Islam and bring it to victory. So he said, "We have named him Harb (War)." Despite being a great warrior himself, this name did not impress the Prophet 🌸, as he preferred to impart mercy and gentleness where possible. Muhammad 🌸 said softly, "He is al-Hasan (The Beautiful One)," and so he was named.

He proclaimed the call to prayer in Hasan's ears and performed an *aqiqa* on his behalf. Just as with Ibrahim, he arranged for Hasan's hair to be shaved and for its weight in silver to be donated to charity. Abu Rafi, the freed slave of the Prophet 🌸 said, "I saw the Messenger of Allah calling the *adhan* into the ear of Hasan ibn Ali when Fatima gave birth." And, in an alternative narration, he said, "The Prophet read Surah Ikhlas in his ear, performed *tahnik* with dates, and named him as well." Then he commanded the legs from the *aqiqa* meat to be sent to the midwife so that she should eat and feed from the same.

From among his family, Hasan resembled Allah's Messenger 🌸 the most, particularly from his head down to his chest. The Prophet 🌸 foretold of Hasan's future and the schism in Islam that he would soon see. In front of everyone, Muhammad 🌸 once said, "Indeed, this son of mine is a *sayyid* (commander). Perhaps Allah will keep him alive and well until he brings peace to two huge parties of Muslims."

Hussain
Only a year after Hasan's birth, Hussain was born on the fifth of Sha'ban. Just as with his older brother, the Prophet Muhammad ﷺ rejoiced in his birth and said, "Show me my son." When he was brought to him, he looked at him with emotion and asked his parents his name. As with his brother, Ali replied again, "Harb (War)!" The Prophet replied as he did for Hasan. Loving beautiful names, he said, "This is al-Hussain (The Little Beautiful One)." The Prophet ﷺ again performed an *aqiqa*, shaving Hussain's hair for its weight in charity. Unlike his brother Hasan, Hussain resembled the Prophet ﷺ from his chest down to his feet, together two parts of the same grandfather.

Allah's Messenger ﷺ loved Hassan and Hussain dearly. He said, "Indeed, Hasan and Hussain are the leaders of youth in Jannah." He would pray for them saying, "O Allah. Indeed, I love them both. Please love them both and love those who love them!" The Prophet ﷺ used to fear that the evil eye would befall them, so he would make *dua* for them repeatedly, saying "I seek you to be protected by Allah's perfect words, from every devil, harmful creature and evil eye."

He would feel a great deal of comfort just from seeing his grandsons and he too would be comforting and kind for them. Once, the Prophet Muhammad ﷺ came out to his Companions carrying his grandsons on his shoulders and kissing them one at a time until he reached his Sahaba. Then he said, "Whoever loves them has loved me, and whoever hates them hates me." Once, Umar ﷺ saw them on Prophet Muhammad's ﷺ shoulders and remarked, "You have a superb horse beneath you." And so the Prophet ﷺ said to him, "And they are two excellent riders!"

In this way, Muhammad ﷺ was always playful with his grandchildren. So many times, the boys would see their grandfather praying in prostration and they would jump onto his back! If a family member wanted to stop them, the Prophet ﷺ would indicate during prayer that they should leave them be. Once he had concluded his prayer, he would place them on his lap with great affection. And, if the Prophet ﷺ was bowing in prayer, he would make sure to widen the gap between his legs to allow his grandson through to join him.

Abdullah ibn Shaddad once reported that Hussain came to the Prophet ﷺ when he was in the company of his people. When he was in prostration, his grandson mounted the Prophet's neck, so the Messenger ﷺ prolonged the prostration so much so that the congregation thought something terrible had happened to him. At the end of his *salah* he was asked, "You prolonged the *sujud*, O Messenger?" He replied, "Indeed, my son was riding me! I didn't want to hurry him."

From all these narrations, we can see that the Prophet ﷺ always took the opportunity to be playful with the young. Once, he was invited to share food with some of the Companions. Hasan was playing in the streets with some of the other children. Allah's Messenger ﷺ raced ahead towards them and spread his arms open, so they ran away, this way and that. Amidst swells of laughter, he finally caught Hussain, then hugged him and kissed him. He was known to say, "Hussain is from me, and I am from Hussain. Allah loves those who love Hussain. Hussain is a tribe by himself from amongst the tribes."

On another occasion, Abu Ayyub al-Ansari came in to see Hasan and Hussain playing in front of, or actually on, the Prophet's stomach. He said, "O Messenger, do you love them?" The Prophet ﷺ replied emphatically, "How can I not love them when they are two sweet flowers from the world and I [only] smell that fragrance?" His kindness reached to the extent that when he saw them once whilst delivering a speech, he noticed that they had stumbled as they walked in, so he stepped down, lifted them up and placed them in front of him saying, "Allah has spoken the truth when He says, "Your wealth and children are tests. Allah possesses great reward. . . I saw these two boys tripping over and I could not hold back, so I concluded my words and picked them up." Such was his affection and dedication to his grandchildren.

One of the leaders from the Bani Tamim, al-Aqra ibn Habis, once saw the Prophet ﷺ kissing one of his grandchildren. Still influenced by the pre-Islamic way of thinking, he found it unbefitting of a prophet to be hugging children. So he asked, "Do you kiss your children? I have ten children and I have never kissed any of them." Muhammad ﷺ replied, "If you do not show mercy, you shall not receive mercy."

But the mercy and love of the Prophet's household did not mean that Muhammad ﷺ detracted from teaching his grandchildren discipline simply because they were young. Hassan once came to his grandfather when he had food to give away as charity. Hassan hurried to some dates in the donations and was about to put one in his mouth when the Prophet ﷺ quickly stopped him saying, "No, no! Did you not know that we are al-Bayt (the Prophet's household), and so we are not permitted to receive charity?"

As well as teaching them etiquette, Allah's Messenger ﷺ would also teach them mercy. And what was more merciful than words of the *witr* prayer? Once, Hassan said,

Allah's Messenger taught me some words I could say in *witr*, "O Allah, guide me with those whom You have guided, pardon me with those whom You have pardoned, take me to Your care with those whom You have taken to Your care, bless me in what You have given me and save me from the evil of what You have decreed. For verily, You command and You are not commanded and none whom You commit to Your care shall be humiliated [and none whom You have taken as an enemy shall taste glory]. Blessed are You, O Lord, and Exalted."

UMAMAH BINT ABU AL-AS

The Prophet's eldest daughter, Zaynab, had a daughter herself called Umamah. She had a special place in the heart of her grandfather, or al-Mustafa, as he was called. He would cherish Umamah, pouring his love and care on her especially, perhaps because of his own unique relationship with her mother. Whilst praying, he would carry Umamah on his shoulders, only placing her down when he bowed or prostrated and lifting her up once again when he stood for the next *rakah*.

Once, Prophet Muhammad ﷺ was presented with a splendid gift, a marble necklace made of rare black and white Yemeni beads. He thought about who he should give it to, perhaps one of his daughters or wives. He declared, "I'm going to pass it to my dearest family member." People presumed he was referring to his dearest wife, Aisha. The women of Medina even said, "The granddaughter of Abu Quhafah, Aisha, will go away with the prize." Allah's Messenger ﷺ surprised them when he called Umama to him. He hugged her, kissed her and breathed her in, as he often used to do with the children from his household. He then smilingly hung the necklace around her neck and marvelled at his radiant grandchild, the necklace only increasing her beauty.

Zaynab, Umamah's mother, had another young child who was sadly struggling with his health. Zaynab sought comfort with her father the Messenger of Allah ﷺ saying, "O Messenger of Allah. My son is on the verge of death. Please be present." He immediately stood up, as did the Companions. Saad ibn Abi Waqqas was amongst them and they all attended Zaynab's home sorrowfully.

When Umamah's brother was raised up to see the Prophet ﷺ, it was clear that death was near. Zaynab held on to the Prophet ﷺ and placed her son on his lap. Muhammad's eyes poured with tears as he watched his grandchild slip away. Taken aback by his tears, Saad said, "What is this, O Messenger of Allah? "He replied, "This is mercy. It has been placed by Allah in the hearts of those whom He wills. Allah does not show mercy but to the kind."

THE PROPHET'S 🌸 STEPCHILDREN

Anas ibn Malik reported, "I never saw anyone nicer to children than Allah's Messenger 🌸." With the exception of Aisha, the Prophet 🌸 married mostly widows or divorcees who all had their own children from previous marriages. He would treat these children like his own and show them special care because without their fathers they were deemed orphans.

They used to live with their mothers under the wing of the Prophet 🌸 who accepted them all in one household. He used to raise them himself, look after them, not dislike anything about them and direct them with politeness when they made mistakes. They used to eat with him, sit with him, and speak to him like they would with their fathers. He was the best of fathers for them, after their own fathers.

KHADIJA'S CHILDREN

Khadija had two daughters, named Hind and Halah, from her first marriage. They grew up under the Prophet's 🌸 wing and loved their stepfather very much. Hind is often recorded describing the personal features of the Prophet 🌸 and once spoke proudly of his household when she said, "I have the best father, mother, brother and sister amongst all people. My father is Muhammad, my mother is Khadija, my brother is al-Qasim, my sister is Fatima. . . who has a family like me?"

UMM SALAMA'S CHILDREN

When the Prophet 🌸 proposed to Umm Salama she already had four children of her own. Trying to excuse herself from accepting his proposal she said, "I have children I am responsible for. I do not wish to neglect them." The Prophet 🌸 sent her a reply saying, "Your family is my family. Your children are dependent on Allah and the Messenger," and so they wed. Muhammad ﷺ cared for Umm Salama's children wholeheartedly, hoping to make up for the loss of their own great father Abu Salama, whom the Prophet ﷺ held in high regard.

Under the Prophet's tutelage, Umm Salama's children were gently taught the correct etiquettes of a good, Islamic child. Her son, Umar, said of his experiences with Allah's Messenger ﷺ, "[When] I was a young child in the house of the Prophet, my hand used to wander here and there on the dining tray. So he said to me, 'Say Allah's name, eat with your right hand and eat what's in front of you.' So I always followed this way of eating thereafter."

Before they joined the Prophet's family, Umm Salama's children experienced their own trials at the hands of the disbelievers of Mecca. Umar's older brother, Salama, spoke once of their difficulties during the Hijra. Abu Salama was one of the first Companions to migrate to Medina. When he left, he placed his wife and their son on a camel. He took the lead, and as they left Mecca both of their families caught sight of them. Umm Salama's family refused to let their daughter leave with her husband. Whereas Abu Salama's family refused to let their grandson go with Umm Salama and started to tug on Salama so violently that his arm became dislocated and he was released from his mother. Abu Salama had no choice but to depart on his own; Salama was held on to by his paternal family and Umm Salama was forcibly separated from both her son and her husband.

Umm Salama was distraught. Every morning for a year she would walk to the site of her separation and weep bitterly. One day, one of her cousins passed by her and felt pity for her. He and others persuaded the families to return her son to her and let her do as she wished. So Umm Salama and her son were finally able to leave for Medina but with no escort to accompany them. When they reached Tanim (a few miles outside of Mecca), they met Uthman ibn Talhah. Although he was not yet Muslim, he was honourable. Uthman vowed to accompany them safely to Medina where the rest of their lives unfolded with Allah's Messenger ﷺ.

SAWDA'S CHILDREN

The Prophet married Sawda bin Zama after the death of his first wife Khadija. Sawda had five children of her own when she married the

Prophet ﷺ, and together they were able to look after the Prophet's children from his first marriage as well.

UMM HABIBA'S DAUGHTER

When the Prophet ﷺ married Ramla bint Abu Sufiyan (also known as Umm Habiba), her daughter Habiba came with her from Abyssinia to join the Prophet's household. History says she lived contently with her mother in the household of Allah's Messenger ﷺ.

THE YOUNG COMPANIONS

ZAYD IBN THABIT

Al-Nawar bint Malik lost her husband during the civil war that took place near Yathrib between the tribes of al-Aws and al-Khazraj. The untimely death of her husband left al-Nawar and her six-year-old son, Zayd, to fend for themselves. Zayd would soon find his place in the world though, as a Companion to the Prophet Muhammad ﷺ. He grew up in his company from a very young age and would always yearn to be near the Prophet ﷺ. Zayd wanted to learn how to pray, how to speak and even how to sit, directly from Muhammad ﷺ himself.

Zayd was also keen to help with the Muslim cause. So in the second year of the Hijra, when the Messenger ﷺ was readying to meet the Quraysh caravan at Badr, Zayd picked up his father's sword and battle gear, eager to enlist. When the Prophet ﷺ saw him, he admired his passion but sent him back to his mother, saying that he was too young to fight. On the army's victorious return from the Battle of Badr, the Prophet ﷺ asked Zayd and a number of other children to learn how to read and write from their prisoners of war. Through teaching the children how to read and write, the prisoners were able to gain their freedom. Zayd excelled in his lessons and his love of knowledge was born.

The following year saw the Battle of Uhud take place, so Zayd asked for a second time to be accepted into the army. With his sword sharpened, he went to the Messenger ﷺ but again returned to his mother disappointed. Zayd's time finally came years later in the Battle of the Trench when he was permitted to bear arms and defend the *ummah*. But despite his eagerness to fight for the faith, Zayd is actually best remembered for his memorisation of the Quran and linguistic capabilities.

From the moment the Prophet ﷺ came to Medina, Zayd heard the words of Allah recited firsthand by the Messenger. Inspired by the revelation, he had a knack for memorising the verses immediately and ultimately became a scribe for the Prophet ﷺ to write down the Quran simultaneously. Zayd persevered until he became one of the few Companions who memorised the entire Quran in the Prophet's lifetime. Not only did Zayd memorise the Quran, he also took the time to understand its complex laws on financial transactions and inheritance. The Prophet ﷺ even declared once, "When it comes to inheritance, the most knowledgeable in my *ummah* is Zayd ibn Thabit."

Despite his young age, Allah's Messenger noticed Zayd's keen intellect, infallible accuracy and strong memory, so he selected Zayd to learn Hebrew on his behalf. The Prophet ﷺ hoped to communicate directly with the Jewish community in their own language and found this a means for ensuring an accurate translation of his statements to them. Zayd started to mix with the Jews of Medina to learn from them. He became quite proficient in Hebrew in a short space of time. Zayd soon became the Prophet's personal translator, and it is related that he learned many other languages too.

After the passing of the Prophet ﷺ, Abu Bakr commissioned Zayd to gather the Quran into a single book. He set about gathering the various parchments, date palms, scapula bone and so on, that had been being used up until this time. Then in the era of Uthman ibn Affan, Zayd wrote out a further five copies for distribution through the major Muslim cities. Zayd transmitted nintey-two hadiths in all and after his youth with the Prophet ﷺ, he ended his days in Medina as the Head of Justice, Recitation of Quran and Inheritance.

ANAS IBN MALIK

The day the Prophet ﷺ arrived in Medina was filled with joy for both young and old. Anas ibn Malik was just 10 years of age, and he narrated, "I never saw a day better, nor brighter than the day the Prophet entered Medina."

To welcome the Prophet ﷺ and to gain his pleasure, many of the Ansar wanted to give him gifts. Umm Sulaim was no different, and she decided to give him her most prized possession, her son, Anas. He was clever with an excellent memory, and he was happy to serve the Seal of the Prophets.

Muhammad ﷺ happily accepted Anas into his household and he therefore grew up under his wing. Day after day, Anas would learn his manners directly from the Quran and Sunnah. He never separated himself from the Prophet ﷺ whilst travelling or at home, and he even attended eight battles during his lifetime. This included the Battle of Badr where, despite his young age, Anas served the Prophet ﷺ personally.

And so young Anas was brought up in the Prophet's household. He was affectionately named Unais (which meant little Anas) and would be delighted whenever the Prophet ﷺ called out to him, "O my little son." Muhammad ﷺ was never harsh with him when he made mistakes, but he would often direct and teach him right from wrong. Once, for instance, he sent Anas on an errand. En route, Anas stumbled on some children and began to play with them, promptly forgetting whatever the Prophet ﷺ had sent him for. Whilst playing in his own world, he felt a hand grab him from behind. It was Allah's Messenger ﷺ smiling and saying to him, "O Unais! Go and do what I told you to do."

Allah's Messenger did not reserve his excellent manners for Anas alone. That was his way with all those who served him and indeed with any vulnerable individuals he met. Whilst others tended to show less concern for such people, the Prophet ﷺ would treat them with extra care and kindness. Anas once said,

> I served the Prophet for ten years in his travels and at home. He never once said, "Uff" to me. Nor did he say about something that I did, "Why did you do that?" He never asked me, "Why didn't you do it like this?" Nor for something I did, "You did that badly." He never criticised me for anything, [even when] I procrastinated, and no one from his family could blame me [for something] except that he would say, "Leave him. If it was meant to be, it would have happened."

The Prophet's generosity extended to Anas' family as well, and he would visit them often, sometimes praying at their house and supplicating for them specifically. Umm Anas even asked him once, "O Allah's Messenger! Will you not pray for your little servant, Anas?" The Prophet ﷺ responded, "O Allah, provide him wealth and children. Bless him and place him in Jannah." Upon hearing this, the best of *duas*, Anas' mother was filled with joy. His *dua* was soon realised as Anas went on to live a long life of 100 years or more. He saw so many of his own children and grandchildren flourish and was the richest of the Companions in both finance and offspring.

As a young servant, Anas would often be privy to many things within the Prophet's household that others could not hope to see. As such, he narrated a total of 2,286 hadiths and would regularly inform others about the domestic life of Allah's Messenger ﷺ. For instance, Anas was once asked about *qiyam al-layl* (night prayer) and he explained, "Whenever you wished to see Allah's Messenger praying, he'd be praying, and whenever you expected to see him sleeping, he would be sleeping."

Every year that Anas matured beside Allah's Messenger ﷺ, he would understand Allah's Messenger more and feel able to ask him very particular things. Once, Anas even asked him to intercede for him on the Day of Jusdgement, to which the Prophet replied, "I'll do that." Zayd asked, "Where shall I find you on the Day of Judgment, O Prophet of Allah?" The Prophet ﷺ responded, "You'll find me first at the Sirat." Anas asked, "If I don't find you at the Sirat?"

The Prophet ﷺ responded, "Look for me at the Mizan." Anas asked, "If I don't find you at the Mizan?" The Prophet ﷺ responded, "Look for me at the Pool."

Anas also narrated that he would refer to him as "my son" when giving him fatherly advice. For instance, once he noticed Anas glancing away during his prayer. The Messenger of Allah ﷺ said, "O my son! Beware of looking around during your prayer because glancing in your prayer is the cause of destruction!" On another occasion, he advised Anas, "O my son. When you enter indoors to your family greet them with *salam*. It will be a blessing for you and on the people of your household."

Anas was only twenty years old when the Prophet's soul was taken. He and the other Companions felt at a loss. Speaking of that day, Anas recalled, "I never saw a day uglier, nor darker than the day the Prophet died. We had barely dusted our hands from burying him when our hearts disliked what we had done."

After the Prophet's death, Anas went on to live in the Levant. He took Basra as his home and was the last Companion to die there. Buried with him is a stick which belonged to the Prophet ﷺ and which

Muhammad had bequeathed to him. Such was his affection for the father-like figure, Muhammad ﷺ.

ABDULLAH IBN UMAR

Abdullah ibn Umar was born in Mecca and actually became Muslim when he was young. Soon after, he migrated with his father, Umar ibn al-Khattab, to Medina. Much like Anas, Abdullah took on many of the Prophet's mannerisms. He had also tried to enlist for the Battle of Badr and Uhud but was turned away for being too young. During the Battle of Uhud though, Allah's Messenger ﷺ permitted Abdullah to be a guard for Medina, alongside Aws ibn Thabit, Aws ibn Uraba and Rafi ibn Khudaij. Again, like Anas, he too was finally permitted to fight during the Battle of the Trench.

Abdullah attended the gatherings of the Prophet ﷺ from an early age. Allah's Messenger quickly noticed that Abdullah was destined for greatness in knowledge and wisdom. He also held Abdullah in high regard because he was the son of Umar, one of the Prophet's senior ministers, and the brother of his wife, Hafsa. As such, the Prophet ﷺ would often address his brother-in-law like an elder and offer him useful advice. For example, Abdullah narrates, "Allah's Messenger held me by my shoulder one day as if he was shaking me to get attention or uninterrupted concentration and said, "O Abdullah. Be in this world as if you are a stranger or a traveller, and consider yourself as a dweller of the graves." Abdullah cared greatly for such advice, and although he was still young, he would practice and transmit these messages to those around him.

When Abdullah was older, the Prophet ﷺ testified to his righteousness and said to his sister Hafsa, "Indeed, your brother Abdullah is a good man. . . if only he observed the night prayer." When these words reached Abdullah, he made night prayer a habit and he never left it again.

It is narrated that Abdullah related 2,630 hadiths from the Prophet ﷺ and that he was the expert on the subject of Hajj. Even from a young age, Abdullah was so knowledgeable in certain areas that he was permitted to issue *fatwas*. He continued to issue such verdicts for a total of sixty years. Abdullah's skills were truly unparalleled in his lifetime, and when he eventually came to rest in Mecca, he was the last of the Companions to die there.

AMAH BINT KHALID

One day, the Prophet ﷺ was brought some clothing. One of them was a small *khamisa*, a black shirt with colourful designs. When the Prophet ﷺ saw it, he realised it would suit a younger person best. He thought of Khalid ibn Sa'id, an early Muslim convert. Khalid was only the fifth or sixth convert in Mecca. He was tortured for it and tried relentlessly in his faith. His own father grew so aggressive towards him that Khalid was forced to migrate to Abyssinia with the other early converts. The sacrifice of these converts was never forgotten by the Prophet ﷺ and he would regularly praise and pray for them.

Allah's Messenger ﷺ recalled that Khalid had a little daughter called Amah. Her family used to playfully call her Umm Khalid. This *kunya* (nickname) stuck with her when she was young. Umm Khalid was born in Abyssinia after her father's migration and she spent her first few years there.

On thinking of Amah, the Prophet's face lit up with happiness. He said to someone nearby, "Bring me Umm Khalid." Her friends and family hurried to tell Amah that Allah's Messenger was inviting them to his gathering - a great privilege. Her mother stood up in a hurry to put on Amah's best yellow garment. She made sure she was presentable and sent Amah with her father to the Prophet ﷺ. When she was brought to him, Muhammad ﷺ took the garment out, put it on her and was delighted with it so much that he said to her twice, "May you remain, may it wear out."

ABU UMAIR

Another child that interacted with the Prophet ﷺ is Abu Umair. He was a young child and lived with his mother Umm Sulaim and his father Abu Talhah, an older Companion who was close to the Prophet ﷺ. Once, Abu Umair was walking through the gardens of Medina with friends. Running between the palm trees, he caught sight of a small yellow finch jumping over the grass. It was a small bird with colourful wings and a red beak. Abu Umair caught it unaware and proudly brought it home.

He became busy with his little pet, enjoying the finch's birdsong and marvelling at the sight of its bright feathers. Abu Umair would feed him, give him water and take care of him. Umm Sulaim was happy to see her son so busy, but sadly this happiness did not last long. One morning, the finch stopped moving. Abu Umair nudged him in the hope that he was just asleep, but there was no response. He called out for his mother and broke down in tears. Allah's Messenger soon visited their home and asked Umm Sulaim, "What happened to Abu Umair?" She replied, "His finch has died, O Messenger of Allah." The Prophet ﷺ said, "O Abu Umair, what's happened to the *nughair* (finch)?"

After seeing the Prophet's concern, Abu Umair felt some relief. But not long after, a worse calamity befell the family. Abu Umair became terribly sick with a debilitating fever. His father, Abu Talhah, was so worried for his son that he became preoccupied with thoughts of him. One day, when Abu Talhah was out, his son sadly succumbed to his illness. His bereft mother prepared the body and placed him safely out of sight. She decided not to tell her husband that evening as she knew how distressed he would be. So when Abu Talhah returned that evening, he found his wife in her finest garments. When he came in, he immediately asked after their son. She replied, "He is calmer than he ever was."

Abu Talhah relaxed, and they spent a pleasant evening together, eventually sharing their bed and sleeping peacefully. The next morning, Abu Talhah had just finished his morning prayer when Umm Sulaim said, "Hope for reward on account of your son. Allah Most High loaned him to us and has now taken him back by His side." Saddened by this terrible news and shocked that his wife had kept this from him, Abu Talhah went to complain to the Prophet ﷺ. However, when he heard what had happened, Muhammad ﷺ simply made *dua* for them both, "May Allah bless you both in the night you spent together."

His *dua* was soon answered, and Umm Sulaim discovered that she was pregnant with her next child. After losing her beloved son, his legacy still remained after her decision to bear the grief alone that day. The story of young Abu Umair and his little finch would always be remembered.

MUATH IBN AFRAN AND MUATH IBN AMR

These two young men from the Ansar had not yet reached puberty but were blessed with courage and strength. They approached Allah's Messenger ﷺ as soon as he arrived in Medina and were immediately filled with love and adoration for him. As two close friends who were hardly ever apart, they would attend the Prophet's gatherings and pray at his mosque regularly. The young boys would listen eagerly to the stories of the migrants who came with the Prophet ﷺ. The Muhajirun would talk about the hardships that the Prophet ﷺ had faced after the start of revelation and his invitation of people to Islam. They told the Ansar of their personal experiences of punishment and torture. The two boys felt a great deal of compassion for their stories. In the stories of unprecedented abuse against the Prophet ﷺ, the name Abu Jahl, in particular, stuck in their minds. After Abu Jahl's relentless attempts to kill Muhammad ﷺ, they decided that he deserved to get recompense for what he had done.

So when Allah's Messenger departed for Badr to intercept the caravan, each young boy grabbed a sword and crept in with the throngs of fighters. The Prophet ﷺ initially went to Badr not to fight but to retrieve money which the Quraysh had stolen from the Muhajirun. However, a battle was forced upon the Prophet, and so his loyal Companions offered him their unwavering support.

Meanwhile, the two young boys agreed amongst themselves to participate in the battle for one objective alone – to kill Abu Jahl. When the two groups faced each other in preparation for battle, they suddenly thought, "But how will we recognise him?" They recognised one of their own men lined up for battle as Abdul Rahman ibn Awf, and so they hurried to his side. Abdul Rahman was surprised and worried that these boys had managed to join them in battle. But before he could ask them how they had come to be there, the first boy asked him, "O Uncle. Do you recognise Abu Jahl?" Cautious as to their intentions, he answered, "Yes, my nephew. But, what need have you of him?" He responded, "We have been told that he used to insult and hurt the Prophet and that he has been planning to kill him." Abdul Rahman confirmed, "That is true." The boy replied, "I swear by He whose hand is my soul that if I see him, my shadow and his will not separate until the one closer to death, dies."

The second boy repeated his friend's words. Abdul Rahman was taken aback and started to look at the two youths with concern. As they were speaking, Abu Jahl strutted out amongst the enemy army. Watching him swagger pompously, Abdul Rahman said to the two boys named Muath, "There, look! Don't you see him? This is the one you have been asking about."

As soon as they could tell who he was, the boys set off, keeping a close eye on their target. Keeping up with Abu Jahl was not an easy task as he was experienced in war. But they continued to follow him, and when he was finally within range, they swooped down on him in attack. Abu Jahl incurred many serious injuries and stumbled to the ground. In his dying state, he was humiliated that his final demise was not at the hands of his peers in battle. Instead, Allah had abased his tyranny and ended his despotism at the hands of two inexperienced youths, Muath ibn Afran and Muath ibn Amr.

UTHMAN IBN ABU AL-AS

Following the Battle of Hunayn, Muhammad ﷺ and his army surrounded the city of Taif. After the battle, many from the opposing army had fled back to Taif, their fortified home town, and a siege began. Having lost many of their own during the battle, the Companions were frustrated with the actions of the Banu Thaqif (people of Taif), and so they asked Allah's Messenger ﷺ to pray for their destruction. But instead, the Prophet ﷺ supplicated for their salvation, "Allah please guide [Banu] Thaqif. Guide [them] and bring them towards you as Muslims."

The siege broke soon after, and a truce was agreed. The Prophet's army left for Medina and the Banu Thaqif decided to send a small delegation from their nobility to meet with him. He received the delegation warmly and set up a tent in the mosque for them so that they could observe the Muslim way of life. Amongst the visitors was a young man called Uthman ibn Abu al-As.

Uthman had a brilliant mind and knew immediately that Islam was his path. He had secretly converted to Islam on his arrival to Medina, unbeknownst to his fellow delegates. So when his companions went to sleep, Uthman would visit the Messenger ﷺ and ask him questions about the religion. He would go to Abu Bakr to develop his understanding of the faith and listen to Ubay ibn Kab's recitation of the Quran. Conversely, the remainder of the delegation took time to come to Islam. They made ridiculous requests of the Prophet ﷺ, asking him to excuse them from *salah* and charity. They even asked to be allowed to commit adultery and consume *riba*. Of course, Allah's Messenger ﷺ rejected all of this and left them to consider Islam as it was. Finally,

Islam entered their hearts and he wrote a letter vouching to protect Taif in their honour.

Uthman's consistent commitment to Islam did not go unnoticed by the Prophet ﷺ. Abu Bakr also praised Uthman and said once, "O Allah's Messenger... this young boy was the most keen and anxious to learn Islam and learn the Quran." Before the delegation departed, Uthman asked the Prophet ﷺ, "O Allah's Messenger, pray to Allah to give me a deep understanding of the religion and to teach me?" The Prophet ﷺ said, "You have asked me something that none of your companions have asked me." That was when Muhammad ﷺ decided to make him the Governor of Taif and their Imam, despite being so young. He told him, "Lead your people in prayer."

Uthman felt overwhelmed and said, "O Allah's Messenger. I find some difficulty in myself regarding this matter." So he said to him, "Come nearer." He placed a hand on Uthman's chest and then said to him, "Turn around." When he turned around, he placed his hand again on his back between the two shoulders and said to him, "Lead your people [in prayer]. Whoever leads their people [in prayer] should pray compassionately, because the elderly are there, the sick and the weak and the person who needs to complete an errand. When [that person] prays alone, he can pray as he wishes." Then he commanded him to place the *masjid* in Taif, where the idols were placed, so Allah would be worshipped where He was not worshipped.

One day, Uthman returned back to the Prophet ﷺ after he had been appointed, complaining, "O Messenger of Allah, verily the Shaytan has come between my *salah* and my recitation, confusing me." The Prophet ﷺ said to him, "That is a devil called Khinzab. When you can sense him, seek refuge with Allah from him and dry spit on your left side three times." Uthman said after, "I did just that and Allah removed him from my mind."

This is the young Uthman who grew up in the shade of Islam. Allah caused his people to benefit enormously from him. When the Prophet ﷺ died, many Arabs left the religion and Uthman's tribe, Banu Thaqif, were considering doing the same. However, Uthman stood amongst his people and said, "You were the last of people to enter Islam, so don't become the first of people to leave it!" So Allah kept them firmly upon the religion.

RAFI IBN AMR

The people of Medina used to take considerable care of their palm trees. They would wait for the fruit to ripen and only harvest their beautiful clusters when they were ready and sweet to eat. So one day, when the farmers saw that somebody had been spoiling their palm trees and looting their fruit, they started a lookout.

They kept an eye on their gardens and suddenly caught sight of a young boy with a strong frame throwing stones at the date clusters so he could eat the dates that fell. Despite warning him away, he persisted, so the farmers wondered what they could do with the young boy. One of the Ansari farmers complained to the Prophet ﷺ saying, "O Messenger of Allah. There is a young man who keeps throwing stones at our palm trees!" They brought the boy to Muhammad ﷺ and the Companions watched closely to see what the Prophet would do.

He didn't fly into a rage, nor did he punish him. True to his prophetic character, he spoke to Rafi gently and asked him, "Young boy. Why are you throwing stones at the palm trees?" The child answered simply, "To eat!" Wanting to explain to him that what he was doing was unintentionally spoiling the trees, he said gently, "Young boy! Do not throw stones at the dates. But eat whatever has already fallen at the bottom." Then he rubbed Rafi's head lovingly and supplicated for him, "O Allah. Make his tummy satisfied!"

That boy grew to be the great Rafi ibn Amr who went on to narrate hadiths of the Prophet ﷺ and fight conquests of Islam before settling in Basra, another child who felt the compassion of the Prophet ﷺ even in his mischievous youth.

LAILA AL-GHAFARIYA

Allah's Messenger once departed for Khaybar, north of Medina, and he passed by the homes of the people of Ghaffar. The women and children caught up with his army and ran to keep up with the rear to offer any services that the warriors might need: nursing, water or food.

Amongst them was a young girl called Laila. She was intelligent and passionate but appeared frail. So the Prophet ﷺ let her sit on a case at the end of his camel's hump to help her keep up. Later in the journey, the Prophet ﷺ came off his camel to rest, as did Laila. When she dismounted, she was embarrassed to see that her first menstruation had occurred and marked the case she had been sitting on. When she saw it, she tried to cover the mark, but the Prophet ﷺ noticed and immediately felt sympathy for her. The Prophet ﷺ did not act differently towards her, instead he hoped to help and advise her. He said gently, "Look after yourself. . . then take a container of water, throw some salt on the stain and wash [it] off. Then return to your riding animal." Laila was not ignored, excluded or ostracized because of her situation. She was shown compassion and offered advice, an approach of which our modern-day communities should take note.

When, by Allah's will, the Prophet ﷺ conquered Khaybar, he gave the women present a portion of the war booty. Laila was fortunate to receive a necklace, which the Prophet ﷺ tied around her neck personally. She was happier than could be and took great care to ensure that the necklace never left her side. As Laila grew up, she contributed whatever she could for the sake of Islam. Towards the end of her life, she even requested that her necklace be buried with her. Another young life touched immensely by the compassion of Allah's Messenger ﷺ.

ABDULLAH IBN ZUBAIR

Abu Bakr al-Siddiq's daughter, Asma, endured a great deal of hardship on her migration to Medina. Her husband was Zubair ibn al-Awwam, and she was pregnant with their child during the journey. The weight of the pregnancy, the arduous journey and the loneliness of the path combined to cause a great deal of worry for Asma. Rumours were also being spread by certain Jewish tribes to cause fear amongst the Muslims. They claimed that they had cast spells on the Muslims to make them sterile so that they would have no offspring and the religion would die out.

Of course, the Muslims knew that this was merely a lie intended to spread animosity, but it still caused concern, even to Asma. She spent her days fearing miscarriage, and so she called out to Allah sincerely in her *duas*. The closer she got to her due date, the more she would pray for her and her unborn child's protection. When her contractions finally began, her family hurried to be by her side. Hearts were soon filled with joyful tears when a strong, healthy baby boy was born to Asma and Zubair. This was the first child born in Medina, and his very existence belied every rumour that had been spread. Voices alternated between praise and thanks. Cries of *Allahu Akbar, Allahu Akbar, Allahu*

Akbar rang out across the city.

The baby boy was brought to Allah's Messenger ﷺ, who received him joyfully and asked Allah to bless him. As he sat calmly on the Prophet's lap, Muhammad ﷺ named the baby Abdullah. We don't know much about how Abdullah interacted with the Prophet ﷺ. But we do know that when Abdullah was roughly seven years old, he came to Allah's Messenger ﷺ, on the command of his father, to pledge his allegiance. The Prophet ﷺ received him graciously, smiled at him, and accepted his pledge.

Abdullah ibn al-Zubair grew up in a unique environment. His father was a close disciple of the Prophet ﷺ and so he was raised on the principles of strength, bravery and fearlessness. Even as a child he was not afraid of others. For instance, Umar ibn al-Khattab would often scare people with his mighty presence. When children saw him whilst playing, they would quickly disperse and leave their games out of embarrassment. So once, when Umar was passing through an alleyway of Medina, Abdullah's friends quickly ran away, leaving only Abdullah standing there. He was not yet 12 years of age. When Umar drew near, he was impressed by Abdullah's fearlessness and said, "Who are you, young boy?" Abdullah replied, "I am Abdullah ibn Zubair."

Umair responded, "May Allah bless you my son. So how is it you did not disperse like your friends you were playing with?" Abdullah did not falter, and he said boldly, "Why should I vanish? I am not a criminal that I should fear your punishment. The path is not so narrow that I have to make space for you." Umar was astonished. Such was the effect of Abdullah's education and upbringing.

When Abdullah grew older, he was of the senior political leaders in Islam. He was made a *khalifa* over Hijaz, Egypt, Yemen, Iraq, Khorasan and most of the Levant. He ruled for nine years until he was tragically killed by al-Hajjaj ibn Yusuf al-Thaqafi. Growing up in the Prophet's presence shaped his outlook and life journey as a whole.

UMAIR IBN SAAD

Umair was a young orphan just ten years of age, when Medina became preoccupied with the Battle of Tabuk. The Prophet ﷺ encouraged the Muslims to spend as much as they could afford towards the battle, in the face of the imminent danger from Rome. While both the wealthy and poor Companions competed to fund this campaign, a group of *munafiqun* were demoralising people around the Messenger ﷺ.

One of those people was called al-Jallas ibn Suwaid, who did not want to leave for Tabuk. He was caring for Umair ibn Saad and was like a father to him. Umair used to love him greatly, but one day al-Jallas said to him, "If what Muhammad has said is true then we are worse than donkeys." Umair was dumbfounded and disappointed with what he had heard. He turned to al-Jallas boldly and said to him, "I bear witness that the Messenger of Allah is truthful and that *you* are worse than a donkey." Al-Jallas was bewildered and embarrassed. He realised that he had hurriedly spoken out of turn in front of the youngster and was immediately worried that Umair would inform the Prophet ﷺ of his words. So he turned to Umair and said, "O Umair. Conceal it for me my son."

The young boy thought about it and found himself between two bitter choices. If he related these words to Allah's Messenger ﷺ he would embarrass al-Jallas, who had helped him a lot by fostering him with care and kindness, but if he remained silent, he feared that would be sinful. Perhaps the Prophet ﷺ would want to know who was demotivating people?

Umair decided he would tell the Prophet ﷺ and hurried to speak with him, despite the fact that al-Jallas was calling him back. Of course, al-Jallas denied that he had said what Umair claimed. Young Umair's position was compromised, so he shed tears and prayed aloud, "O Allah, send down upon the Prophet a clarification of what I have spoken about." The gathering went quiet, and in that moment a revelation was indeed revealed. The Prophet ﷺ raised his head and recited,

> [The hypocrites] swear by God that they have said nothing [wrong]; yet most certainly have they uttered a saying which amounts to a denial of the truth, and have [thus] denied the truth after [having professed] their self-surrender to God: for they were aiming at something which was beyond their reach. And they could find no fault [with the Faith] save that God had enriched them and [caused] His Apostle [to enrich them] out of His bounty! Hence, if they repent, it will be for their own good. but if they turn away, God will cause them to suffer grievous suffering in this world and in the life to come, and they will find no

helper on earth, and none to give [them] succour.

(Quran 9:74)

Umair was elated and relieved. Al-Jallas said simply in a quiet voice, "Ask my Lord to accept my repentance, O Messenger of Allah." The Messenger ﷺ turned to Umair and touching his ear he said, "Your ear has performed well Umair. Your Lord has confirmed your honesty." Another child's life was immeasurably changed by the example and the kindness of the Prophet Muhammad ﷺ.

AFTERWORD

In this age of modernisation and globalisation, the duty of teaching our children *tarbiyah* has never been more important. If our children are lacking in *tarbiyah*, the household will crumble from the inside out. And if a child doesn't feel satisfied by good practice in his or her own home, they will inevitably look to outside influences for guidance. Sadly though, the household no longer provides a safe haven to protect a child's religious and cultural identity. The key principles of such identity were traditionally transmitted by the older generation to our young, and social expectation promoted adherence to their norms.

The role of the mother and father has also changed. The respect, love and comfort that parents were once associated with has now lost its place in society. Parents no longer know how to relate properly to their children and only seek to please them without receiving true affection in return. Children often deride their parents as 'out of touch' and the gap between the generations only widens because of it.

The duty of parents today is a huge undertaking in both education and self-development. The most important tool they can provide their children with is to be a righteous role model themselves. Both parents must commit to moral uprightness and refrain from anything that tarnishes that. But how?

To begin with, we need to clean our homes of negative behaviour. Remove the lying, emphasising of other's mistakes, consumption of haram, neglect of prayers and so on. Instead, we must fill our spaces with positive acts by prioritising knowledge, devotion to Allah, cooperation, fear of the Almighty and personal development. In doing so, that house will be more wholesome, letting our children, and indeed wider society, reap the benefits.

Happy were the children who were raised around the Messenger ﷺ, the Companions and their successors. Most, if not all, of them became great people. Why? Because they found a purpose in their life and received a nurturing upbringing from the role models that surrounded them, particularly the Prophet Muhammad ﷺ. With the solid foundation of a society that adhered to Islamic principles whilst also offering a loving environment to its youngest members, these children found their footing in the world.

Indeed, in that is a reminder for whoever has a heart or who listens while he is present (in mind). (Quran 50:37)

O Allah, benefit us with what you have taught us, teach us what benefits us and increase us in knowledge. *Ameen.*

APPENDIX
General Habits and Sayings of the messenger ﷺ around Children

Allah's Messenger ﷺ shared the experiences of his young companions throughout their daily lives. He would be delighted when they were joyful and he would feel dismay when they were in pain. He would teach them but also persevere in learning alongside them. Here are some examples from the Prophet's life that shed a little more light on his interactions with children, and some of his recommendations or sayings regarding childhood.

- Whenever a child was born, the Companions would bring the baby to the Prophet ﷺ for him to pray for them. They would seek his supplication and blessings, and he would perform *tahneeq*.

- Every child has been pledged to have an *aqiqah*. So on the seventh day, a sacrifice is given on his behalf, his hair is removed and he is given a name.

- If children entered the house of the Prophet ﷺ and he had some dates, he would grab hold of some, give them to the children and stroke their heads in welcome.

- Abdullah ibn Ghudar once said, "My mother sent me to Allah's Messenger with a bunch of grapes and I ate a few on the way. So he held my ear in jest and jokingly said, 'O traitor!' "

- The Prophet ﷺ saw a man walking with a young boy. He asked the young boy, "Who is this man?" The boy replied, "He is my father." The Prophet ﷺ said, "Then do not walk ahead of him, don't insult him, don't sit before he does and don't call him by his name."

- Once, the Prophet ﷺ was riding a camel with his cousin, Fadl ibn Abbas, riding behind him. It was the day of sacrifice on Hajj and Fadl had just reached puberty. Fadl started to look at a beautiful woman whilst she was talking to the Prophet ﷺ about matters of faith. So the Prophet ﷺ held Fadl's chin and turned his face away to stop him staring. Fadl said, "You have turned your nephews neck away!" The Prophet replied, "I saw a young man and a young woman. I have to safeguard them from tribulation."

- The Prophet ﷺ said on the subject of prayer, "Command your children to pray at the age of seven. When they are ten you can hit them for it and separate their beds too." Note, 'hit' here refers to hitting without causing any bodily harm or injury to the child and avoiding the face. *It is important to note that the Prophet himself never hit a woman, a child or an animal.

- On the subject of gifts to children, the Messenger of Allah ﷺ said, "A parent never gave a better gift to his child than good manners." And he also advised on equity between children, "Be equal when you give presents to your children. If I was to favour anybody, I would favour women."

- "Whoever has a daughter and he didn't bury her alive, he didn't humiliate her and he didn't favour his son over her, he would enter Paradise."

- A son approached his father, so the father placed him on his lap and kissed him. His daughter then came too, but he sat her in front of him. The Prophet ﷺ said, "Won't you treat them equally?"

- "It is a sufficient sin for a person to neglect those who are dependent on him for food."

- "I and the sponsor of an orphan will be like these two fingers." He then made a gap between his forefinger and his middle finger.

- "The first words you should start your children on are *la ilaha illa Allah*."

- Allah's Messenger ﷺ met a caravan in Rawha. A woman raised up a child and asked, "Can this child perform Hajj?" The Prophet replied, "Yes, and the reward for it will be yours."

- Rabi bint Muawaz reported that Allah's Messenger ﷺ sent a message to villages of the Ansar in the early morning of Ashura saying, "Whoever has entered this morning fasting, then complete the fast." Rabi said, "We used to fast that day thereafter and encourage our children to do so too. We used to give them a woolen toy. If they cried for food, we'd give that to them until it was *iftar* time."

- "If a child knows his right from his left then command him to pray."

- "Teach your children three qualities: love for the Prophet ﷺ, love for the Prophet's household and recitation of the Quran. The reciters of the Quran will be under the shade of Allah's Throne on a day when there will be no shade except for His shade, with His prophets and His chosen elite."

- "The right of a child over his father is that he should teach him the Book, swimming and archery and that he should only provide what is pure and wholesome for him."

- "Don't supplicate against yourselves, don't supplicate against your children, don't supplicate against your servants and don't supplicate against your wealth. You won't coincide with a specific hour of supplication to acquire something except that you will be granted what you wanted."

- "If I stand up to pray intending to prolong it and I hear the crying of a child, I repeal my intention in case it inflicts hardships on his mother."

- Asad ibn Wadaa reported that a man called Juzay came to the Prophet ﷺ and asked, "Indeed my family disobey me. How much should I correct them?" He said, "Pardon them." Then he repeated it a second time and then a third. Finally, he said, "If you punish, only do so according to the disobedience and avoid the face."

- "Indeed, Allah does not have mercy on the ones who do not show mercy to their children. I swear by the One who has my soul in His Hand, only a merciful person will enter Paradise."

- On the authority of Umar ibn Salama, his delegation asked, "O Allah's Messenger. Who should be our Imam?" He replied, "The one who has learned the most Quran." They put me forward while I was still a young boy. In every gathering I was their Imam."

- "None of you believe until I become dearer to him than his parent, his child and the whole of mankind."

- "Tests will continue to befall a believing man and woman in his family, children and wealth until he meets Allah without a single sin."

ALSO AVAILABLE BY LIGHT PUBLISHING

www.ingramcontent.com/pod-product-compliance
Lightning Source LLC
Chambersburg PA
CBHW011959090526
44590CB00023B/3784